POSITIVE WORDS,

POWERFUL RESULTS

SIMPLE WAYS TO
HONOR, AFFIRM, AND
CELEBRATE LIFE

HAL URBAN

A FIRESIDE BOOK
PUBLISHED BY SIMON & SCHUSTER
New York   London   Toronto   Sydney

FIRESIDE
Rockefeller Center
1230 Avenue of the Americas
New York, NY 10020

For information about special discounts for bulk purchases,
please contact Simon & Schuster Special Sales:
1-800-456-6798 or business@simonandschuster.com

Designed by Jan Pisciotta
Manufactured in the United States of America

1   3   5   7   9   10   8   6   4   2

Library of Congress Cataloging-in-Publication Data
Urban, Hal, 1940–.
Positive words, powerful results: simple ways to honor, affirm,
and celebrate life / Hal Urban.
p. cm.
"A Fireside Book."
1. Success. 2. Conduct of life. 3. Psycholinguistics. 4. Thought
and thinking. I. Title.

BJ1611.2.U73 2004
177'.2—dc22   2004041760

ISBN 0-7432-5769-3

This book is dedicated to the best person I know

RUTH URBAN

Mom,
your words of
love and encouragement
continue to bless and enrich my life.

Kind words can be short and easy to speak, but their echoes are truly endless.

—MOTHER TERESA

Contents

x CONTENTS

PREFACE

There's Nothing New Under the Sun . . .

What has been will be again,
what has been done will be done again;
there is nothing new under the sun.
Is there anything of which one can say,
"Look! This is something new"?
It was here already long ago;
it was here before our time.

—ECCLESIASTES 1:9–10

. . . or in This Book

One of the observations that many readers of my first book, *Life's Greatest Lessons,* made was that I didn't try to sell them a "startling and new" formula for permanent success and total happiness. Instead, they expressed their appreciation for the way I'd pulled together some simple truths that had been around for a long time and presented them in a logical, commonsense manner that helped people get back on the right track. The CEO of a large insurance firm called and told me, "What you wrote about is so old it's revolutionary." And then he added, "But we need to be reminded about these old truths because too often we get sidetracked and forget about what's really important." I really liked that man. I liked him even more when he bought a book for every employee in his company.

Hundreds of people have made similar comments, and each one was taken as a compliment. Because shedding new light on old truths was exactly what I was trying to do. Now I'm trying to do it again. You probably won't find anything new in this book about words and the way we use them. You'll just be reminded that what you say, and how you say it, can, indeed, be important. Even life changing.

> *The world does not require so much to be informed as to be reminded.*
>
> —HANNAH MORE

INTRODUCTION

Two Simple Reasons for Writing This Book

1. TO INCREASE AWARENESS OF THE IMPACT OUR WORDS CAN HAVE

We live in an ocean of words, but like a fish in water we are often not aware of it.

—STUART CHASE

The above statement was written in 1953 by a scholar who conducted extensive research on the power of words. Much has changed since then. There are about a billion more people, the literacy rate has risen dramatically, countless new methods of communication are available to us, and we've added thousands of new words to our vocabulary. So the ocean of words we live in today dwarfs the one we lived in during the 1950s. But some things never change. We seem just as unaware of their impact today as we were fifty years ago. Maybe more unaware.

I think this is so because we so often take things for granted. Words are tools that we've always had access to and have used every day since we started talking. Because they've always been there and because we use them so frequently, we get into verbal ruts. We often talk without thinking first and without being aware of the impact of our words. Yet they can have a powerful impact—both on others and on ourselves.

Kahlil Gibran, the much-loved poet from Lebanon, wrote more than thirty years ago that " . . . in much of your talking, thinking is half murdered." Again, I don't think much has changed. "Put your mind in gear before putting your mouth in motion" is one of those timeless axioms that we too often forget. I hope to offer several practical reasons here for honoring it and for teaching and helping others to do the same. We need it more than ever.

2. TO ENCOURAGE THE USE OF WORDS THAT CELEBRATE AND AFFIRM LIFE

I can live for two months on one good compliment.
—MARK TWAIN

It's been said that language is an index of civilization. What we hear all around us every day literally speaks volumes about our culture, our ethos, and our consideration for one another. I'm not alone in my belief that much of the language we've been hearing for the past thirty years has tarnished that civilization.

In the late 1960s, people were urged to "let it all hang out," and they've been doing just that, particularly with words, ever since. Much of the language we hear today has a harshness to it. To be more specific, it's often crude, angry, and mean-spirited. We hear it just about everywhere we go and it comes from people of most age groups.

Keep in mind that I said our civilization has been tarnished, not destroyed. What it needs is some tender loving care and a little polish. And I'm just optimistic enough to believe that we can apply that polish with a better choice of words.

Shortly after the first George Bush was sworn in as president in 1989, he was asked what his vision was for the country. He said he wanted America to become a "kinder, gentler" nation. Many people, regardless of political persuasion, were in agreement. But what happened? His comment was belittled and made fun of in the media. Only proving, of course, that we really *did* need to become a "kinder, gentler" nation. I still think it's possible, and a good way to start would be to use kinder, gentler words.

That's the theme of Chapter 10 in *Life's Greatest Lessons*. It's called "Kind Words Cost Little but Accomplish Much." I knew shortly after the first edition was published in 1992 that I wanted to expand on that particular lesson. Since then I've been listening, reading, conducting little experiments, and collecting anecdotes in order to support my theory that the words we use have a great impact on our lives . . . and on our society. So, in many ways, this book is an enlargement of that chapter, along with the ones on humor, respect, and thankfulness—three more ways we can use words to enhance lives.

Another experience has further convinced me to build on that theme. Since 1995 I've been speaking at schools, conferences, businesses, and places of worship about the relationship between good character and the quality of life. A major part of each of those presentations is about the power of kind words. In fact, I'm often asked to give keynote addresses about that specific topic. Each time I do, the response is overwhelmingly positive. It's a hopeful sign.

In the preface to my first book I wrote the following: "I hope you will become part of the growing movement to return us to a society known for its civility, virtues, and old-fashioned goodness." The best tool we have for doing that is our language. It contains thousands of wonderful, positive, and life-affirming words. They're readily available, they're free, and we can use them any time we want. I encourage you, as I remind myself, to do it often. It's fun, it's positive, and it's rewarding. Our kind words *can* make a difference.

> *Never believe that a few caring people can't change the world. For, indeed, that's all who ever have.*
>
> —MARGARET MEAD

Gentle Words

What the dew is to the flowers,
Gentle words are to the soul,
And a blessing to the giver,
And so dear to the receiver,
We should never withhold.
Gentle words, kindly spoken,
Often soothe the troubled mind,
While links of love are broken
By words that are unkind.
Then O, thou gentle spirit,
My constant guardian be,
"Do unto others," be my motto,
"as I'd have them do to me."

—POLLY RUPE

PART ONE

THE ORIGINS AND INFLUENCE OF WORDS

Speech is civilization itself.

—THOMAS MANN

The instruments of both life and death are contained within the power of the tongue.

—PROVERBS 18:21

Chapter 1

Words Make Us Human

Words are what hold society together; without them we should not be human beings.

—Stuart Chase

When Did We Start Talking?

I've always wanted to believe that the first word ever spoken by a human was "yippee!" Something good was discovered and a sound came out to celebrate it. Someone with a less positive worldview might think the first word was either "darn" or "ouch." But the truth is, no one knows for sure which human uttered the first word, exactly when or where it was said, or what it meant.

Anthropologists can give us all kinds of scientific data on the origins of the human race, but they can't tell us with certainty when we started talking. It's not my intent here to write a historically documented or scientifically proven account of the development of language, and I suspect that it's not your desire to read one. But it might be useful briefly to discuss the origin of words.

Every species of animal on the planet has a system of communication. And every linguistics professor on the planet agrees on one point: Our language is what sets us apart. It's what makes us distinctly human. Many of our day-to-day functions are the same as those of the family dog or the pig at the county fair: eat, drink, sleep, reproduce, survive. But because we think at a higher level, we developed a more sophisticated system of communication called language. Within it thousands of words have emerged. We use them to connect with one another and to give meaning to our experiences.

Our Hands Came First

Most of us have had the experience of trying to communicate with someone who doesn't speak English. While it's stressful and a bit frustrating, we're usually able to send some clear messages. We do it mostly with our hands by pointing and making other gestures, and with our facial expressions. It's called body language. This was the first method of communication used by our ancestors.

Try to imagine going through each day of your life without being able to speak to those around you. That's what early humans had to do. The hands and the face were effective tools of communication, but they too often came up short in articulating needs and feelings.

A case in point: A few years ago my wife, Cathy, and I were in Rovaniemi, Finland. It's a small town near the Arctic Circle, and not too many people in that remote part of the world speak English. We arrived in the afternoon, and after exploring the city for a few hours, returned to our hotel for dinner. There we noticed a local man sitting at the bar, which was actually part of the lobby. He didn't speak English, but it was clear that he wanted to welcome us to his community. It was also clear that he wanted to do this by buying us a beer. At this point he *was* speaking our language. It had been a long day, we were tired and thirsty, and we accepted his gracious hospitality.

Then came the hard part. This man desperately wanted to have a conversation with us, but we had learned how to say only "hello," "good-bye," "please," "thank you," and "bathroom" in his language. That pretty much limited our conversation. But he was determined. He repeated the same sentence over and over, but we had no clue what he was trying to tell us. Each time he made his statement, he spoke a little slower and a little louder, as if that would help us better understand what he was saying. It began to dawn on us how incredibly funny this scene was. We also wondered how many beers he had had before we joined him. But as funny as it was, we didn't dare laugh. It would have been inappropriate if he was trying to make a serious point with us.

Not laughing when something is funny added to not understanding what another person is telling you is a double dose of stress. It began to wear us out. We finished the beers and drew on a few of those words from our five-word Finnish vocabularies: "thank you" and "good-bye." We made gestures to tell him that we enjoyed the beer and that it was time for us to eat dinner. We shook hands with him and went to the dining room with big sighs of relief. No wonder the early inhabitants of Earth developed a language. It was our first stress reducer.

PICTURES CAME SECOND

Our ancestors must have also grown tired of just pointing and getting excited looks on their faces. They wanted to communicate in more specific ways. So next in the process was the drawing of pictures. Whether people had great artistic talent or not, they learned that they could send a message with a more precise meaning by sketching drawings on the ground or on cave walls. Even the stick figures I draw probably would have worked.

The people in ancient Egypt were particularly effective at advancing this form of communication. Sometime before the year 3100 B.C., they came up with an advanced system of pictures that became known as hieroglyphics. The word itself means pictorial characters. At first they were purely picture symbols, but in due time they came to be used conceptually also. For instance, the symbol for "sun" eventually came to mean "day," and the symbol for "moon" came to mean "night."

This was obviously moving us in the direction of a language. Pictures and symbols were far more descriptive than hand signals and grunts, but it took a long time to draw them. We needed something more efficient. Then along came the Phoenicians.

WORDS CAME THIRD

If you ever wondered where the term "phonetic spelling" or the word "phonics" came from, now you know: the Phoenicians. These people from the eastern Mediterranean, along with the Greeks, gave us the roots of the modern alphabet. From it came words and the development of a language, regarded by many as one of the greatest achievements in the history of the human race. Speaking words replaced drawing pictures as the primary way of communicating with one another.

What *is* a word? That's a question I always asked my students. For many years I taught a course in communication at the University of San Francisco. At the same time I was teaching a course in the psychology of personal growth and development to high school students. One of the major components of that course was a unit called "communication and relationships." Whether teaching the adults in my university class or the kids at the high school, I always started with the same question: "What is a word?" And I always got the same two responses: puzzled looks and the question, "What do you mean?"

What I was trying to do was get my students to examine more closely the real meaning and significance of words. I asked if they had ever looked up the word "word" in the dictionary. None ever had. So I asked them, "How would *you* define 'word'?" I got more puzzled looks and then some awkward attempts to define these sounds we use in our daily process of connecting to the world. While not many students came up with a good definition, they did become intrigued with the issue. They started asking questions like, "What *is* a word?" and "How *do* you define it?" I was pleased. My primary goal as a teacher was always to get my students to think.

The dictionary offers several definitions of "word." I read two of them to my classes: (1) "a speech sound that symbolizes or communicates a meaning . . .," and (2) "a verbal signal." Then I challenged them to come up with their own definition, one that was easy to understand and agreed upon by everyone in the class. I asked them to think about what they were really trying to do each time they used a word. I also suggested that looking for a good synonym for "word" might get them to zero in on what it really is. In all the classes I taught on this subject, the two best synonyms for "word" that my students came up with were "symbol" and "sign." I always asked them, "What about 'picture'?"

PAINTING VERBAL PICTURES

We talk to others and to ourselves in words, but we *think* in pictures. Example: If I say the word "tower," you'll form a picture of one in your head. If I say "Eiffel Tower," you'll form an even more precise picture, unless you've never seen it or a photo of it. What we're doing most of the time when we're talking to another person is exchanging pictures. As we've added words to our vocabularies, our language has become more sophisticated. It's like adding colors to an artist's palette—we can now paint more vivid pictures with our words.

I did an exercise with my students at the beginning of each course to show them just how vividly we think in pictures, even when we're not conscious of it. I told them I was going to say a word, and I wanted them *not* to form a picture of it in their minds. I said, "No matter how great the temptation is, *do not* form a picture. By now they were wondering where I was going with this, but they were game. I asked them if they thought they could do this simple little exercise. They were confident they could.

I said, "Okay, ready, . . . one . . . two . . . three . . . the word is . . . truck." The class immediately burst into laughter. They realized that, even when they were trying not to, they formed pictures when someone else was talking to them. When I asked them to describe their trucks, I got all kinds of vivid descriptions—fire engines, four-wheel-drive pickups, monster trucks, tow trucks, etc. And every student in the class could tell me what color his or her truck was. All of this detail when they were trying to *not* form a picture. Whether you realize it or not, every time you talk to another person, what you're really doing is sending pictures back and forth. It's more specific than gestures and faster than hieroglyphics.

What do good teachers and good speakers do? They paint vivid verbal pictures. They do this by telling good stories to make their points. That was one of the first things I learned when I started my teaching career. During my first year in the profession, one of the outstanding teachers at my high school told me, "If you're a good storyteller, you'll be a good teacher. You'll get a lot more across with a story than you will with a lecture." That was some of the best professional advice I ever received. They say "a picture is worth a thousand words." A good story paints a thousand pictures.

Words and Culture

The point of this little history of words is to show how they've developed over the years and to remind us how important they've been throughout history and how vital they are in every culture. Words are what we use every day of our lives to connect with the world and the people in it. They're the tools we use to greet, inform, ask, answer, teach, encourage, comfort, praise, celebrate, thank, pray, laugh, and connect in a myriad of other positive ways.

We can, of course, also use words in a variety of negative and hurtful ways. While the focus of this book is on positive words, there's one chapter about negative words. It's here because we need to increase our awareness of the damage our words can do and be reminded that we can take control of our tongues.

I've been asked many times in recent years if I was going to write a sequel to *Life's Greatest Lessons*. While that may be done in the future, this book was written to share one of the most powerful lessons I've ever learned: Kind words cost little but accomplish much. They can even change lives.

Life and language are alike sacred.
—Oliver Wendell Holmes

Words

They sing.
They hurt.
They teach.
They sanctify.
They were man's first,
immeasurable feat of magic.
They liberated us from ignorance
and our barbarous past.

—LEO ROSTEN

CHAPTER 2

WORDS CAN CHANGE LIVES

Throughout human history, our greatest leaders and thinkers have used the power of words to transform our emotions, to enlist us in their causes, and to shape the course of destiny. Words can not only create emotions, they create actions. And from our actions flow the results of our lives.

—ANTHONY ROBBINS

THE TONGUE AND THE PEN ARE MIGHTY

Words have shaped history. They've given birth to ideas, started wars, inspired millions, and made people rich and famous. Words can hurt and shock, or they can heal and lift spirits. They can even get us to buy things. Words can change lives, for better or for worse. King Solomon said, "Death and life are in the power of the tongue," and a familiar saying tells us that, "The pen is mightier than the sword." Words are not only powerful, but they can have a lasting impact.

What kinds of feelings come with these words?

destroy	kill	hurt
jail	explode	forbid
suffer	ruin	rape
hate	fire	terror
damage	unemployed	stupid
beat	idiot	shoot
crash	injure	worry
riot	criticism	stress
agony	death	sue
revenge	disease	poison
murder	embarrass	war
prison	stab	gloomy
steal	hit	arrest
jerk	cheat	bitter
bum	lie	threat
mean	tragedy	burn
lose	flunk	complain
scam	jealous	evict
avoid	battle	sad
drugs	dispute	warning
condemn	break	tension
spit	strangle	force
ugly	fat	dumb
corrupt	cancel	assault

What kinds of feelings come with these words?

love	warm	party
friend	vacation	puppy
kindness	weekend	good
peace	play	success
forgive	hope	fairness
joy	home	beauty
fun	courage	agree
happy	faith	confidence
win	calm	kiss
reward	nice	hug
improve	child	grow
smile	profit	praise
laugh	celebrate	wonderful
alive	funny	deserve
enthusiasm	secure	invite
respect	positive	heal
achieve	affection	cure
comfortable	thankful	gracious
trust	champions	leader
entertain	achieve	tribute
honor	comedy	blessed
baby	support	smart
fresh	help	heaven
truth	strengthen	special

If I asked you to select any five words in the list on page 12, and then asked you to form pictures in your mind that go with them, would they be pleasant ones? Probably not. If I asked you to write sentences using any five of these words, would they be positive statements? Probably not. But if I asked you to select any five words in the list above, then form pictures and write sentences about them, it's highly probable that the results *would* be pleasant and positive.

This is a little experiment I've been doing with my students and people in my workshops for several years. I gave out the page with negative words first and just asked them to look at it for a few minutes. Notice that one of the words on it is "tension." In a short time, that's exactly what there was in the room. Yet just before I handed out that page, there was plenty of positive energy in the room and everyone seemed to be in a good mood. This one page of words seemed to cast a pall over everyone. Then I asked them to form the five pictures and write the five sentences. Things get worse. One adult student said, "This is a downer." Another wanted to know *why* we were doing it. He said, "I thought you wanted us to be positive." I answered that I did, but that I also wanted to teach them something about the emotional impact of words. A third student said, "You succeeded, but now we all feel crappy." And because they knew me so well, a fourth student asked, "Can we assume that there's going to be a page of positive words also?"

That was my cue. I smiled smugly and handed it out. The entire atmosphere in the room changed. There was animated conversation and laughter, and the positive energy returned. In fact, it seemed to be higher than it had been before we started the exercise. Then we did the pictures and the sentences, and things got even livelier. One of my more insightful students said, "Words have more impact than I thought, and these are just on paper."

If a piece of paper with words on it can lower or raise the spirits of more than thirty people within seconds, think of the effect that some of the words we speak can have on others . . . and on ourselves.

What Research Tells Us

There's been a vast amount of research conducted on the influence of particular words. Trying to summarize all of it here would be fruitless, but I do want to share the findings of two interesting

studies that support the claim that words can have a powerful
effect. The first one comes from the advertising industry, that seg-
ment of our society that seems to study the impact of words even
more than linguists do. Why? Because certain words have been
found to work like magic on consumers. As I stated earlier, words
can get us to buy things. Go into your local supermarket, stroll
down the aisles, and watch them pop out at you. You also hear
them in television and radio commercials and see them in newspaper and magazine ads. Here are some of them:

you	proven	love
easy	health	guarantee
new	money	save
results	safety	discover

According to research conducted in business schools at several
top universities, these are twelve of the words most likely to influence a prospective buyer. One business even managed to get
eleven of them into one marketing slogan: "You will love to save
money with Germ-Gone, the easy-to-use, proven new discovery
that guarantees your health and safety." There was no evidence to
indicate whether the product or the slogan worked successfully.

David Ogilvy, a well-known man in the field, writes in his
book *Confessions of an Advertising Man* that there are several additional words that have also tested positive for working on consumers. Here are some of them:

miracle	magic	quick
improved	bargain	hurry
revolutionary	amazing	offer
wanted	now	sensational

The point of all this is to show that words, when used strategically, can have a decided effect on the people they're aimed at. If

words, when carefully selected, can get people to buy things, then they also can be used to reach people in many other ways. The keys are to be more aware of their likely impact and to select them with greater care.

The second study worth mentioning here strongly suggests that words can even affect our physical health. Research was conducted by the National Institute on Aging on the impact of certain words that reinforce stereotypes about people over the age of sixty. If words like "senile" and "decrepit" and jokes about failing memory and aches and pains are regularly used around seniors, they'll have an adverse physical, as well as psychological, effect. Blood pressure will rise and nervous reactions will often appear on the skin. On the other hand, if words like "insightful" and "wise" are used around seniors while communicating to them that they're valued, the results are much the opposite.

Fairly new to this age group myself, I've chosen not to let negative labels like "slow," "old," "losing it," "fading," and "fossil," even when people are supposedly kidding, get to me. But they obviously *do* get to many seniors, and the research suggests that we should use more life-affirming words when in their presence. Why not describe these people in my age group as educated, active, kind, worldly, experienced, fun-loving, appreciative, valuable, and contributing members of society?

Actually, it doesn't make any difference which age group is studied regarding the impact of words. The truth is that words can tear down and words can build up no matter how young or old we are.

WORDS CAN CHANGE LIVES

One of the questions I frequently ask people I meet on airplanes is "Has a person ever said anything to you that changed your life?" I could fill this book with the wonderful stories I've heard.

It's amazing how much people will open up to a complete stranger, especially when they find out that he's collecting information for a book. Interestingly, all of the answers I received were about positive words that brought about positive changes. I heard heartwarming stories about the kind, loving, and encouraging words of parents, grandparents, teachers, coaches, friends, bosses, pastors, etc. And in most cases, the person who said the inspiring words had no idea how powerful or long-lasting they would be.

To make my point about how seemingly simple words can change lives, I've chosen two stories. The first I read in a newspaper, the second one I experienced firsthand.

FOUR WORDS THAT CHANGED A LIFE

A few years ago I was in Chicago's O'Hare Airport and picked up a copy of the *Chicago Tribune*. A column by one of its well-known writers, Bob Greene, caught my eye immediately. It was called "Four Words That Changed a Life." He began the article by explaining a scene he had recently witnessed in a public place. A mother was obviously upset with her young son and asked him in a loud voice, "Are you too stupid to do anything right?"

Greene's observation of this incident caused him to think not only about the impact of this woman's words but also about how long it would last. He writes, "Not a big moment, perhaps. Yet small moments sometimes last a very long time. And a few words, though they mean little at the time to the people who say them, can have enormous power. 'Are you too stupid to do anything right?' Words like that can echo." Greene's comments strongly support a couple of the main points in this book. To begin with, we need to be more aware of the effect that our words might have on someone else. We also need to understand that words we often utter carelessly or while in an emotional state can have a lasting impact.

Greene points out that positive words can also have a major influence and can last a lifetime. His story is about a professional writer who was shy and lacked confidence in his childhood. But something happened in his high school English class that changed his life. It was a routine occurrence—his teacher returned a writing assignment to him. He doesn't even remember what the grade on that paper was, but he does remember the four words she had written on it: "This is good writing."

This was a young man who liked to write and often dreamed of composing short stories, but he lacked the confidence until that day. His teacher's little note got him to think differently about his abilities, and it was the beginning of a successful career in writing. To this day he believes that it would never have happened without those four words written in the margin of his paper. Greene concluded his article this way: "So few words. They can change everything."

THREE WORDS THAT LAUNCHED A BOOK

Life's Greatest Lessons almost died in its infancy. One of the biggest disappointments of my life occurred when the original publisher informed me that the book was being taken out of print. It was both shocking and disheartening. The book had sold out of its first printing and I was receiving wonderful feedback from readers. It was exciting, and I couldn't help wondering how many copies would be printed on the second run. Then came the bad news.

After wallowing in self-pity for a few hours, I decided to look at my options. The feedback from readers and their requests to buy more copies were encouraging, so I didn't want the book to die. At the same time, I had no clue as to how I might obtain more. "Out-of-print" has a pretty final ring to it. I called the publisher and asked if there was some way I could get more books. I was told that the company could have more printed for me, but that I'd have to buy a minimum of two thousand copies and pay for the shipping. My original thought was, "It's over."

It was a simple matter of economics. I was a high school teacher who had to moonlight to make ends meet. In addition, my three sons had just completed college, and our life savings had been seriously depleted. It would be just about gone if I bought the two thousand books. Also, I was never the entrepreneurial type. I didn't take risks with money, and this seemed like a big one. What if I bought the books and couldn't sell them? I'd have no savings and a garage full of worthless merchandise.

That evening Cathy came home from work and I shared the bad news about the book going out of print and the additional bad news about how expensive it would be to buy more. Since she knew the state of our savings, I figured she would say something like, "No way!" But she didn't. Instead, she said three words that changed everything: "You'll sell them."

It's impossible to explain just how powerful Cathy's words were. Simply put, her words got me to think differently. They inspired me. We had a long discussion about it, and at the end, we decided to buy the books. I sold the two thousand, then bought another two thousand and sold them. After that I went into self-publishing, and total sales surpassed eighty thousand before the book was sold to Simon & Schuster. In announcing the deal, *Publishers Weekly* called it "the little book that could." It makes for a nice story, but there wouldn't have been one to tell without Cathy's three encouraging words.

"So few words. They can change everything."

Words have the power to destroy or heal. When words are both true and kind, they can change our world.
—BUDDHA

The Power of Words

—

A careless word may kindle strife.
A cruel word may wreck a life.
A bitter word may hate instill.
A brutal word may smite and kill.
A gracious word may smooth the way.
A joyous word may light the day.
A timely word may lessen stress.
A loving word may heal and bless.

—AUTHOR UNKNOWN

Chapter 3

Words Can Hurt and Offend

"Careful with fire" is good advice we know.
"Careful with words" is ten times doubly so.
—WILLIAM CARLETON

Why This Chapter Is Necessary

When I set out to write this book, I was determined to keep it entirely upbeat and positive. But the farther I got into outlining it, the more I realized that this chapter not only couldn't be avoided but was absolutely necessary. If one of the goals in writing the book is to help us become more aware of the impact of our words, then we need to take a good look at the many ways we might say something that's hurtful or offensive. An increase in awareness can help keep us from damaging others as well as ourselves.

In my previous book there was a chapter on the importance of honesty. There, also, I wanted to focus solely on the positive—the rewards of being a person of integrity. But it was impossible to effectively point out those rewards without also pointing out the consequences of dishonesty. This is somewhat similar. Part of the process of becoming a person who's wise with words and one who affirms life in others is learning to avoid saying those things that have the opposite effect. This chapter is actually nothing more than a brief refresher course on those types of things we want to avoid.

FREE SPEECH IS GOOD— OFFENSIVE LANGUAGE ISN'T

Before I discuss the ways our language can be offensive, I want to comment on something I've heard many times: "This is a free country. I can say anything I want. Haven't you ever heard of free speech?"

The First Amendment to our Constitution is one of the most important documents ever written. Freedom of expression is the very bedrock of a democratic society, and it's one of the main reasons we've achieved greatness as a country. While I strongly favor free speech and just as strongly oppose censorship, I also favor good taste, consideration for the feelings of others, and what used to be called common courtesy.

THE DIRTY THIRTY

"What kind of language drags you down? What are some of the things you don't like to hear other people talk about?" These are two questions I've asked people of all ages literally hundreds of times in the past several years. I asked them in my classroom, in workshops, on airplanes, and in casual conversations. I simply told people that I was conducting research for a book about the power of words, and they were more than willing to contribute. I explained that I was working on a section about the kinds of things we don't like to hear, things that either hurt us, offend us, or drag us down.

While the responses didn't surprise me, they did serve as a wake-up call in two ways. First, they reminded me just how many ways there are to poison the atmosphere with our words. Second, it was with some embarrassment that I viewed the list, realizing that I was often guilty of using some of these methods. It helped me make a conscious effort to eliminate as many of them as I could. I hope it will do the same for you.

Here's what people say they don't like to hear. I call them the "Dirty Thirty."

1. Bragging
2. Swearing and other gross-out language
3. Gossip
4. Angry words
5. Lies
6. Mean-spirited and hurtful words
7. Judging others
8. Playing "poor me"—the self-pity game
9. Making discouraging remarks
10. Embarrassing and humiliating people
11. Excessive faultfinding and criticism
12. Complaining, moaning, whining
13. Rude and inconsiderate language
14. Teasing
15. Manipulation
16. Trying to impress others with phony and insincere comments
17. Ethnic and racial slurs
18. Sexist comments
19. Age-related put-downs
20. Being negative—always pointing out what's wrong
21. Threats
22. Arguing
23. Interrupting—not letting the other person finish

24. Playing "trump"—always topping someone else's story
25. Being a know-it-all
26. False flattery
27. Yelling
28. Talking down to people—being condescending
29. Exaggerating
30. Blaming and accusing others

THE FLAGRANT FOUR

Over the years, I've asked my students and the people who attend my workshops which of the Dirty Thirty are the most frequently heard, which seem to be tarnishing our culture the most. They consistently chose these:

1. Swearing and gross-out language
2. Complaining, moaning, whining
3. Mean-spirited and hurtful words
4. Rude and inconsiderate language

I want to comment here briefly on the first three and address the fourth in Chapter 9, "Gracious Words Show Respect and Gratitude."

SWEARING AND GROSS-OUT LANGUAGE

The majority of Americans . . . wonder at the effluence of raw language and worry about its impact on old-fashioned notions of civilized discourse.

—RICHARD CORLISS

A few years ago, I took my copy of *Time* magazine out of the mail and was somewhat dismayed, but not shocked, to see the lead story. On the cover was a drawing of a large mouth with guns, knives, bombs, flames, and other deadly symbols coming out of it. The cover had "DIRTY WORDS" in large bold letters at the top, along with the subheading, "America's Foul-Mouthed Pop Culture."

On the inside, the story is called "X Rated," and it begins with these words: "It's a four-letter world out there: in rock and rap, in movies and on TV, in comedy clubs and real life. Many love it, especially kids. Many others hate it or don't get it." The story goes on to tell us what we already know: Foul words are a big part of our entertainment industry and consequently have become part of our everyday language as well. We are what we are because of what goes into our minds.

To give you an idea about just how much things have changed, let me share a story from my many years in a high school classroom. During the first twenty years I taught, foul language was never a problem. If a student slipped and let out with an obscenity, I would ask him (girls didn't swear in those days) a simple question: "Do you talk like that in front of your parents?" The answer was always no. Since the California Education Code says the teacher is *in loco parentis* (Latin for "in the place of the parent"), I simply requested that there be no swearing in front of me, either. My students never had a problem with that.

But sometime during the 1980s, that began to change. The answer was yes when I asked students (both the boys and the girls) if they spoke that way in front of their parents. They often added, " . . . and they talk that way in front of me, too." This meant that I had to drop my old reliable question and get a new one. I did, and it worked right up through my last year of teaching in 2001. The new question was, "Are there any places you go in which you don't swear?" They all had some of those places, so the answer was always yes. All I had to do was add, "And now you have another one—my classroom."

As both a father and a teacher, I always tried to be realistic and practical on the language issue. I was raising three young sons at home and spending all day with teenagers, and I wanted to help all of them deal with this new social problem. Since I'm neither a prude, a bluenose, nor a right-wing zealot, I didn't think preaching about the evils of bad words would accomplish anything. But teaching about decorum, civility, and courtesy would.

I asked them a series of questions that always provoked both thought and some excellent discussion:

- Would you think differently of me if I constantly used swear words?

- Would it lower the standards and damage the atmosphere of my classroom?

- Do educated and cultured people talk this way?

- Do people in important positions of leadership use this kind of language?

- Are there places in our society in which you don't want to hear swear words?

- Do you think some people might be offended when they hear those kinds of words?

- Are people who use foul language in public polite or rude?

- What do you reveal about yourself when you constantly swear?

They got it. What really helped them understand was their own answers to the last question. Here's what these teenagers said about people who constantly use foul language:

- They're angry.
- They're uneducated.
- They're rude and inconsiderate.
- They have limited vocabularies.
- They aren't creative or imaginative.
- They're clueless.
- They have filthy minds.

Even the kids who admitted to swearing a lot said this exercise got them to think about what they were saying about themselves. A significant number of them said, "I know I swear way too much. It's become a bad habit." A significant number of them also told me later that they were proud of the fact that they had changed their language patterns for the better. They hadn't stopped swearing completely, but they had cut it down significantly, especially in places where it might offend someone else.

COMPLAINING, MOANING, WHINING

I personally think we developed language because of our deep inner need to complain.

—JANE WAGNER

Most people have no idea how often they complain. The reason is that we live in a culture of complaint. It's going on all around us all the time. Why, when we have so much for which to be thankful? My own theory is that the more we have and the easier life is, the more we complain. We take so much of what we have for granted that we start sniveling as soon as things are less than perfect.

To put you in touch with your complaining, let me give you a little assignment that I first gave my high school and university students in 1972 and now give to both kids and adults in my speaking audiences. By a conservative estimate, I've given it to more than eighty thousand people. It's called the Bruce Diaso Memorial Challenge. Here it is: Starting right now, go the next twenty-four hours without complaining . . . about anything! What did my students do when I gave them this assignment? They complained that it was too hard!

How many people have been able to do it? A grand total of five. It took twenty-three years to find the first one. As I write this, I'm still on the hunt for more. Of the five, two were high school kids, one was a seventh grader, one was a fourth grader, and one was an adult. This means one out of every sixteen thousand people who were given the assignment was able to complete it successfully. I tried to measure the percentage, but it was too small. Thousands of people refused even to try it. Why? "Because it's impossible to go a whole day without complaining," many of them said.

The important question is, did the people who tried it learn anything of value? An unqualified yes! Here's what they've been telling me for more than thirty years:

- I complained within the first ten minutes.
- I can't believe how hard it is to not complain.
- I had no idea that I complained that much.
- Everybody complains too much.
- What I complain about is stupid. I shouldn't even be complaining about so many piddly little things.
- Complaining is just a habit.
- I need to stop complaining so much.

Let me give you a little background on the origins of the assignment and why it's called the Bruce Diaso Memorial Challenge. Bruce was a classmate of mine at the University of San Francisco, and to this day he's one of the most amazing persons I've ever met. Bruce was paralyzed by polio as a senior in high school just before the Salk vaccine came to his hometown of Fresno. When he arrived at USF, he was in a wheelchair. The only parts of his body he could move were his hands (but not his arms) and his head. Inside that head was a great brain and inside his heart was a great disposition. And no one *ever* heard him complain.

All of us were in awe of how upbeat Bruce was. I asked him one day at lunch how he managed to be so positive all the time. His answer was simple, wise, and profound. He said, "I didn't want to live the rest of my life feeling sorry for myself or being angry, so I decided to be thankful instead." I was a little embarrassed, but I had to ask him what he was most thankful for. He said, "God, my family, my church, my friends, the university, my teachers, the brain I've been given, and a life full of opportunities." I received a solid education in the classrooms at USF, but what I came away with from that casual lunchtime conversation was probably the most valuable lesson I ever learned: Focus on the good in life . . . and be thankful for it.

Bruce went on to graduate with high honors, earn a scholarship to law school, and return to Fresno for a successful career as an attorney. Sadly, his career and his life ended too early. He died when he was only thirty-one. His frail body just gave out. But Bruce left a great legacy because he touched the lives of everyone who met him. I'll remember him for a lot of reasons. One is that he was the most thankful person I ever knew. He taught me to focus on the good in life and to be thankful for it. Another is that I never heard him complain about anything in all the years I knew him. Can you do that for even one day?

*   *   *

MEAN-SPIRITED AND HURTFUL WORDS

Sticks and stones can break my bones, but words can break my heart.

—ROBERT FULGHUM

This is, without question, the single most difficult and uncomfortable part of this book to write. There are two reasons. The first is that it's about something I find truly abhorrent: using words as if they're weapons, using them to deliberately inflict pain on other people, sometimes considerably injurious and long-lasting pain. The second is that it conjures up some disturbing memories about times when we've been hurt badly by someone else's careless or deliberately mean words. I apologize if this hits some sore spots in your memory bank, but I think it's important that we grow from these painful experiences. If we're mindful of how much someone's words hurt us in the past, we'll be less likely to do the same to another person. The great Confucius advised us thousands of years ago not to do to others what we don't want done to ourselves. This sage advice included not hurting each other with words.

Is this kind of hurtful language more prevalent now than in the past? Recent polls tell us yes, and a significant number of respected sociologists confirm it. They tell us it's happening for a variety of reasons. Chief among them is the entertainment media. Beginning in the late 1960s, movies became more "real" with the use of raw language. That seemed to open the floodgates. It eventually spread to television, comedy, and the music industry. And along with what we used to call "dirty" words came verbal violence—putting people down with harsh language. This actually became a form of entertainment. We now hear it almost every time we turn on the TV, even during many of the prime-time sitcoms. I guess this means that it's "funny" to put people down, to hurt them, to humiliate them.

Another reason for the increase in cruel language is the increase in stress levels. In our high-tech, pushbutton, multitasking society, millions of people are trying to do too much while depriving themselves of sleep, rest, and time for reflection. These are the same people who seem to be always in a hurry, have frazzled nerves, and are ready to snap at any moment. They get frustrated, then they get angry, then the venom starts flowing from their mouths. The victims are many. We hear this kind of language every day—in stores, at work, in families, in schools, at sporting events, in airports, in cars—just about everywhere.

Unfortunately, most of us have been on the receiving end of this kind of verbiage. It hurts a lot more than sticks and stones do. Some words have a way of penetrating our psyches. They get in there, cause great injury, and often leave scars that take a long time to heal. I urge you, with all the passion I have, to learn to control your tongue, especially when you're in an emotionally charged situation. Once you say something, you can't take it back. And those words that only took seconds to utter can cause pain that lasts for years.

. . . a deceitful tongue crushes the spirit.

—PROVERBS 15:4

CORRECTING OURSELVES— BENJAMIN FRANKLIN STYLE

I've been fascinated with Benjamin Franklin since reading his autobiography while a history major in college. One of the things he wrote about that left its mark on me was the method he used for eliminating bad habits. He would write a list of the behaviors he wanted to change in a small personal journal. Then at the end of each day he would put a dot in the journal for each time he did the very thing he was trying to avoid. His goal, of course, was to go several weeks without having to put any dots on the page.

I tried this as an assignment pertaining to the Dirty Thirty with both my high school and university students, and it worked remarkably well. After showing them the list of thirty not-so-nice things to say, I asked if anyone in the class struggled with at least a few of them. The answer I heard most often was, "More than just a few." I asked them to select the three they would most like to stop doing. Then I gave each of them three index cards and asked them to write one of the bad verbal habits at the top of each card and enter the date. The instructions were to carry the cards with them and place a dot on the appropriate one each time they said the thing they were trying to not say. We did this for five consecutive days. I say "we" because I did it along with them.

While not every student took it seriously, the ones who did said they benefited greatly from it. They found out how difficult it is to break habits (especially verbal ones), they enjoyed the challenge, and they made significant progress in achieving their goals. I had used the method before, but never pertaining to language. It was trickier than I thought it would be, but I managed to dramatically increase my own awareness of verbal choices and eliminate some unpleasant things that seemed to be coming out of my mouth more regularly than I had realized.

A few additional notes about the Dirty Thirty. To begin with, none of us is perfect, and we shouldn't beat ourselves up when we make a mistake, verbally or otherwise. If we can reduce those mistakes, and improve on the way we talk to others, we're making progress. Second, there are times when we need to offer criticism, when we have every right to complain, when expressing anger is appropriate. The important thing is that we learn to do

these things at the right time and in the right way. As for the
other twenty-seven on the list, we would do well to eliminate
them.

> *The real art of conversation is not only to say the right*
> *thing in the right place, but far more difficult still, to*
> *leave unsaid the wrong thing at the tempting moment.*
> —DOROTHY NEVILL

King Solomon
on
Words That Hurt and Offend

Put away perversity from your mouth; keep corrupt talk from your lips. 4:24

. . . Violence overwhelms the mouth of the wicked. 10:11

. . . Whoever spreads slander is a fool. 10:18

Reckless words pierce like a sword. . . . 12:18

. . . He who speaks rashly will come to ruin. 13:3

A scoundrel plots evil, and his speech is like a scorching fire. A perverse man stirs up dissension, and a gossip separates close friends. 16:28

He whose tongue is deceitful falls into trouble. 17:20

A fool's lips bring him strife, and his mouth invites a beating. 18:6

A fool's mouth is his undoing. . . . 18:7

FROM THE BOOK OF PROVERBS

CHAPTER 4

WORDS COME FROM THE HEART

For a man's words will always express what has been stored in his heart.

—LUKE 6:45

OUR WORDS REVEAL US

Several years ago, a wiser and older friend told me, "Every time we open our mouths, we reveal something about ourselves." He said it during one of our many discussions in which he informally mentored me. I was going through one of those "down" times that life occasionally deals out, but thought I was doing pretty well at keeping it to myself. He pointed out that I wasn't. He said our conversations always started out positive, but it was only a matter of time before I began expressing frustration and anger. In a gentle way, he helped me understand that our words are usually a reflection of what's going on inside.

Robert MacNeil, of the *MacNeil/Lehrer NewsHour,* says that when we examine our own language, we get to know ourselves better. This man who has used words so successfully in his distinguished career said his first great lesson in the relationship between self-knowledge and words came from reading S. I. Hayakawa's classic book, *Language in Thought and Action.* He praised Hayakawa for showing us how to use our language "to make us less belligerent, less fearful, more cooperative, more reasonable people." He says that these lessons learned about language have helped him in both his personal and professional life. He points out the wisdom offered by the famous oracle at Delphi—"Know Thyself"—and says we can accomplish this by taking a closer look at our own language.

FREUD ON WHAT WORDS REVEAL

Sigmund Freud has probably been the subject of more jokes than any person in history. Whether you think he was a loony, a great scientist, or something in between, he did get us to look at ourselves differently by teaching us about our subconscious minds. He also taught us that what's going on inside has a way of slipping out verbally. Hence, the Freudian slip.

Freud experimented with a variety of techniques in trying to help his patients get to the root of their psychological problems. One was intense psychoanalysis; another was hypnosis. But his greatest discovery happened by accident. He found that by just talking to his patients in a free-flowing conversation, the truth would eventually slip out. This is one Freudian theory on which most psychologists agree. The main point here is that our words, even when we're trying to hide our feelings, reveal what's stored inside.

STORED IN THE HEART OR IN THE MIND?

People often use such terms as "speaking from the heart" and "heartfelt thanks." I've often wondered about these kinds of expressions because the heart is an organ that pumps blood, while the mind is where we actually store information, feelings, etc. But "speaking from the mind" and "mindfelt thanks" don't exactly do the job. We've been using the heart as a symbol for deep feelings for so long now that it's become an official part of our vocabulary. The dictionary gives us several definitions of "heart," and one of them is "the emotional or moral as distinguished from the intellectual nature." Others are "one's innermost character, feelings, or inclinations" and "the central or innermost part." So the heart really is the place where we have all of our words stored.

WHAT'S IN STORAGE . . .
AND HOW DID IT GET THERE?

If what comes out of our mouths is the overflow of what's stored in our hearts, it would be wise to take a good look at the source. We need to examine the words that have been spilling out, or are about to. But more important, we need to ask ourselves how they got there in the first place. What kinds of words are going in?

We're being constantly bombarded by messages and information almost everywhere we go: people talking, billboards, radio, TV, newspapers, books, magazines, music, the Internet, e-mail. I don't know if anyone has ever done a scientific study on it, but I couldn't help wondering how many thousands of words go into our minds every day.

To give you an idea, a person talking steadily, such as a college professor or a preacher, says about six thousand words in just one hour. Admittedly, we're not listening to lectures and sermons all day (although it probably seems like it at times), but think how many words are being pumped in on the average day. I became so intrigued with this question that I did an informal and very unscientific study of my own. For one week I counted, estimated, and tallied the words I heard and read. It came out to more than forty thousand per day. That's a lot of input.

Obviously, the vast majority of those words do their proverbial thing—go in one ear and out the other. But a lot of them have staying power, especially the ones we hear over and over. Those are the ones we're most likely to use when we talk to others. Because they will, indeed, slip out. Since the main point I am making in this book is that kind, affirming, and encouraging words can make our world a better place, we might want to make sure that the hearts from which our words spill over have something good in them.

Can We Control What Goes In?

You are what you are because of what goes into your mind.

—Zig Ziglar

Zig Ziglar is a well-known motivational speaker and author from Texas. I've always appreciated and enjoyed him for a number of reasons. He's wise, positive, funny, reverent, and full of common sense. He also has some great sayings that get right to the heart of the matter. One of his best and wisest is the one above. I had it on a sign in huge letters in the front of my classroom for many years. One of the reasons I displayed it prominently is that it's the best statement I ever found about the significance of an education. I'm not talking about just formal education, but *all* education. We truly are what we are because of what goes into our minds.

But I had it there for an even more important reason. Almost every day I reminded my students that we were being deluged from all sides with a torrent of words. The pictures those words represent get into our heads and have a strong effect on the way we think and the way we talk. Obviously, we can't control all the messages we're blitzed with, but we have more control than we think. We can do two things to make sure our hearts are full of good words.

1. SCREEN OUT THE TRASH

The first time I heard Zig Ziglar speak in person many years ago, he said several things that got my attention. One of them was a question: "Would you let someone come into your home and dump a big bag of trash all over your living room?" I don't think anyone in the audience knew where he was going at that point, but he made it clear with his next question: "If you wouldn't let someone dump trash in your living room, then why do you let them dump trash into your minds?"

He went on to explain the many sources from which words come flying at us every day and the powerful effect they can have on us. He also reminded us that by simply paying more attention to our input, we can easily screen out much of the negative. We can change TV channels and radio stations, we can close offensive reading materials, and we can avoid, at least to some extent, being around people who drag us down with their glum conversation. In other words, we *can* eliminate a lot of the negative input.

2. START THE DAY WITH POSITIVE INPUT

The friend and mentor whom I mentioned at the beginning of this chapter taught me something valuable on the same day he told me that our words always reveal what's going on inside. In fact, I would call it one of my own "life's greatest lessons" because it's affected me daily in a positive way for more than thirty years.

He said he started every day by putting something good into his mind. He got up about twenty minutes earlier than he needed to, and before turning on the radio or the TV or looking at the newspaper (all of which were bound to have bad news), he sat down in the quiet of the morning with a cup of hot coffee and something uplifting to read. He said it had a positive effect on him for the remainder of the day, which included the things he talked about. He added that he'd done this for so long he couldn't imagine starting a day any other way.

It was probably the next morning that I started doing the same thing. The effect was so astounding I was immediately hooked. I found that feeding my mind with something positive each morning got my day off to a good start by putting me in the right frame of mind. It affected not only my thinking but also my talking for the rest of the day. It's one of the best habits I have. Now that it's my turn to be a mentor, I often urge others to do the same.

During the first few years that I did this I read books by motivational speakers Zig Ziglar, Denis Waitley, Og Mandino, Robert Schuller, and several others. It was like getting a pep talk every morning with positive and fresh ideas to carry with me throughout the day. I also read in the field of psychology, particularly works by the "human potential" specialists like Abraham Maslow, Carl Rogers, Rollo May, and Leo Buscaglia. They all had a very optimistic view of human nature, and it was helpful to start my day with them. I found myself often wanting to share what I read that morning with my students, so it became an extension of my teaching. They used to ask me how I could be so positive and cheery, especially in the morning. I told them I started each day with a "start-me-up breakfast." "What's that?" they asked. My answer was, "Coffee, a bagel, and inspiration."

During the past several years, the content of my morning reading sessions has changed significantly, but it still sets the tone for my day and influences how I talk. I now read from the Scriptures and from books written by authors like Thomas Merton, St. Augustine, Harold Kushner, C. S. Lewis, Max Lucado, and others who explore our spiritual nature. I find these readings both soothing and encouraging, and they get my day off to an even better start. I still have the "start-me-up breakfast," but now it's coffee, a bagel, and wisdom.

GIGO refers to the way computers function. It stands for "garbage in, garbage out." It's acutally simple logic. But this common phrase can also apply to human beings. And GIGO can stand for something else: "good in, good out."

Good, the more communicated, more abundant grows.
—JOHN MILTON

When you meet your friend
on the road side
or in the market place,
let the spirit in you
move your lips
and
direct your tongue.

—KAHLIL GIBRAN

CHAPTER 5

WORDS ARE CHOICES

Respect the power of words. Choose them with care.
—CHINESE FORTUNE COOKIE

CONSCIOUS OR UNCONSCIOUS?

There's a chapter in my first book about making choices. It's called "We Live by Choice, Not by Chance." The main point was to remind us that we're making choices all the time, but we're often unaware of it. One of the important choices I pointed out in that chapter has to do with how we treat other people: "We can put them down, or we can lift them up. We can be self-centered and inconsiderate, or we can be respectful, kind, and helpful." For the most part, we do these things with the language we choose.

I recently got a reminder about making choices with our minds and our mouths from an unexpected source: a TV infomercial. I was doing my "male thing" of flipping through the channels when a rather colorful guy appeared on the screen. Because he was interesting and different—part bodybuilder, part huckster, part psychologist—he got me to stick around for a few minutes longer than normal. I've always found psychobabble entertaining, and this guy had a truckload. Here was a weight-lifting, tan Adonis who kept referring to himself as "Doctor" while flexing his muscles and pushing a weight-loss program. He said, "I'm going to help you make better choices." Then he turned up his volume and asked, "Do you realize that every single thing that goes into your mouth is a CHOICE?"

I flipped to the next channel when he started pitching his particular brand of food products, which he called "the right choices." But I was thankful for the brief visit because he got me to think about something important: Not only do we choose what goes *into* our mouths, we choose what comes *out* of them. But again, we're not always aware that we're making choices. Tony Robbins, a well-known speaker and author on personal achievement, says, "Most of us make unconscious choices in the words that we use; we sleep-walk through the maze of possibilities available to us."

MAYA ANGELOU ON CHOOSING WORDS

Maya Angelou is one of my all-time heroes because she can do with words what few others can. She's used them to write best sellers, win the Pulitzer Prize, and get invited to read one of her poems at a presidential inauguration. One of the reasons she's so skilled at using words effectively is that she's keenly aware of their power. In an interview with *USA Weekend* magazine a few years ago, she said, "I am convinced that words are things, and we simply don't have the machinery to measure what they are. I believe that words are tangible things, not ephemeral . . . that words, once said, do not die." In that same interview Ms. Angelou also made one of the most compelling statements I've ever read regarding the impact that our choice of words can have on others:

* * *

Words go into the body. So they cause us to be well and hopeful and happy and high-energy and wondrous and funny and cheerful. Or they can cause us to be depressed. They get into the body and cause us to be sullen and sour and depressed and, finally, sick.

Let's examine this statement a little more closely. It tells us that our words "go into the body" of another person and can make him or her feel

- hopeful
- happy
- high-energy
- wondrous
- funny
- cheerful

But if we choose different words, they also "go into the body" of that other person and can make him or her feel

- sullen
- sour
- depressed
- sick

Which type of words do we want coming into our own bodies? Which type of words do we want to put into the bodies of those around us? These are important choices, and we make them every day.

Realize now the power that your words command if you simply choose them wisely.

—ANTHONY ROBBINS

Daily Communication Choices

If you asked my students, whether at the high school or at the university, what some of the life lessons were that I emphasized the most, many of them would answer in one word: "choices." I told them at the beginning of every course that they were always making choices, and I reinforced it every day. I also had a big, bright orange sign on the wall in my classroom that had nothing on it except that one word: "CHOICES." Even when I wasn't talking about it, they were seeing it in front of them.

I also started every communication course with a simple exercise that helped increase my students' awareness. It was called Daily Communication Choices. They were asked which option in each pair was the better one:

Complain	Express appreciation
Swear	Use clean language
Lie	Tell the truth
Tear people down	Build people up
Use rude words	Use polite words
Ignore people	Greet people
Gossip	Not gossip
Take people for granted	Tell people they're valued
Laugh at someone	Laugh with someone
Blame someone	Accept responsibility
Talk about yourself	Ask about others
Point out things that are wrong	Celebrate things that are right
Leave people's names out ("Hi")	Say their names ("Hi, Chris")
Discourage others	Encourage others
Demand things	Request things
Use angry words and tone	Use gentle words and tone
Be sarcastic	Be sincere

Talk while others are talking	Listen while others are talking
Avoid eye contact	Make eye contact
Be straight-faced	Smile

It won't surprise anyone that the choices made by both the kids and the adults were overwhelmingly from the right column. The better choices were so obvious that some of the students were calling them "no-brainers."

But making the choices on paper while in a controlled environment like school and actually *doing* them in our day-to-day lives are two different things. I asked them if they had ever made any of the "bad choices," such as lie, gossip, swear, use sarcasm, put others down, etc. They all had. I asked if there was anyone in the class who had *never* made any of the "bad choices." There was no one, and that included me. Then the predictable happened. Someone would always say something like, "Yeah, but we didn't realize we were making choices." I loved it! That was the whole point of the activity, and we always ended it with a valuable discussion about how words are, indeed, choices. My students also agreed that we say way too many things without thinking. We frequently make unconscious choices of words.

GREETINGS ARE A CHOICE

One of the areas in which we frequently make these unconscious choices of words is in greeting others. Does the following sound familiar?

Jim: "Hi, Bob. How are you?"
Bob: "Hi, Jim. I'm fine. How are you?"
Jim: "Fine."
Bob: "Good."

Now, there's certainly nothing wrong with that common exchange between two people. It's probably repeated millions of times each day and usually in a friendly manner. But it's also done a bit mindlessly and has now become our standard greeting ritual. Do we really want to know how people are, or do we just want to hear them say "fine" so we can move on? In most cases it's the latter.

Several years ago I came to the conclusion that every greeting has in it at least four wonderful opportunities: (1) to be a bit more imaginative and creative, (2) to have fun, (3) to lift someone else's spirits, and (4) probably lift our own. During an average year at the high school, I had about 170 students. Since I met each one of them at the door before every class, I gave and received 170 greetings a day. There were handshakes, hugs, high fives, low fives, knuckle bumps, and a variety of other ways they chose to greet me. And each one came with a warm verbal exchange. It was incredibly energizing to start each class this way.

At the beginning of each year, I would get the standard "How are you?" from about ninety percent of my students. But they didn't get the standard "Fine" in return. I had a variety of answers, but my favorite was, "Well, I was good. But now that you're here, I'm even better!" Because it was an unexpected response, it usually provoked some laughter. And because I genuinely loved teenagers and was sincerely happy to see them, my answer also brightened their day. It was always a win-win situation.

I also had a variety of questions that I asked them when we greeted. I tried to avoid the standard "What's up?" and "How's it goin'?" Instead, I asked "SP" questions, which I also taught them to ask. "SP" means "strategically positive." It means the question is specific and will always elicit a positive and specific answer. Here are a few examples of SP questions:

- Who's someone you're thankful for? Why?
- What's been the highlight of your day so far?
- What's the best place you've ever been?

- What's an important goal you have?
- Who's your best friend? Why?

In all, my students and I developed more than a hundred questions. We found that they accomplished a number of things: The questions made the other persons feel important, the answers always led to more good questions, and the conversation that followed was always positive and upbeat. They're simple and they work. How we greet others is a choice. Good greetings make for better relationships, increased energy, and more fun.

THREE CHOICES THAT INFLUENCE OUR WORDS

1. Tone of voice

It's not so much what you say,
as the manner in which you say it.
It's not so much the language you use,
as the tone in which you convey it.

—AUTHOR UNKNOWN

Many social psychologists claim that up to forty percent of our verbal communication is made through tone of voice. It can at times be even more than that. Voice inflection is at the heart of everything we say—it puts feelings behind our words. There are volumes of research to support this, but the findings can be reduced to something we already know: Tone of voice can be as important as, sometimes more important than, the words we use. They're both choices.

We can choose to store good words in our hearts and we can choose to say all kinds of life-affirming things to other people. But along with those choices we need to make another one—*how* we're going to deliver our message. This is where empathy comes in. It's one of the most important ingredients of effective communication. When we're able to put ourselves in the place of those we're talking to, we're far more likely to make a good connection. Empathy helps us choose the right tone.

2. Body language

Our bodies are "talking."
—DAVID WEST

Those same social psychologists who tell us that tone of voice can be forty percent or more of our communication go even higher with body language. They say we often use our bodies to express more than half of what we have to say. While body language isn't as popular as it was in the 1970s when a series of books came out on it, experts on communication are in agreement that our bodies have a lot to "say." They also suggest that if we want to be effective communicators, we should be particularly aware of our facial expressions and how we use our hands.

I learned early in my teaching career, and later as a speaker, that one's delivery is just as important as the content. In fact, if the tone and body language aren't right, the message won't get through. These are also choices we make each time we talk to another person. Smiles and friendly gestures are great companions for kind words.

3. Touch

If you want to get closer to those around you, be aware of the power of communication which you hold in your hands.
—ALAN LOY MCGINNIS

California has a reputation for having a lot of New Age, touchy-feely people. Please don't conclude that I'm one of them. I do often touch people when I'm talking to them, but it has nothing to do with where I live. A gentle touch or an affectionate hug, tendered in an appropriate setting, can be a powerful way to strengthen our words. Just as the right choice of tone can make our kind words softer, the right choice of touch can make them warmer.

For a long time the skin was looked upon as nothing more than a covering for the body. But extensive research in both biology and psychology has taught us differently. Alan Loy McGinnis, an author and family therapist, says, "More than half a million sensory fibers flow from the skin through the spinal cord to the brain. As a sensory system, it is the most important organ of the body." This is the main reason that gentle touching is part of therapy. It can stimulate people who are starving for affection. McGinnis adds that "when it is a genuine expression of your affection, touch can bring you closer to another than can thousands of words." Think what kind words, a soft tone, and a gentle touch can do when combined.

ANOTHER CHOICE—
SOMETIMES SILENCE IS GOLDEN

Wise men talk because they have something to say. Fools talk because they have to say something.

—PLATO

It is better to remain silent and be thought a fool than to speak and remove all doubt.

—ABRAHAM LINCOLN

Maybe these two men have told us everything we need to think about. Sometimes not saying anything is the wisest decision. But how many times have we spoken up without thinking and then regretted it later? It's because most of us haven't received enough instruction and training in communication to teach us to pause reflectively, listen attentively, develop empathy, and think before we talk. But we can learn these important skills in a variety of ways: books and tapes on communication skills, specialized training, college courses, and the best way of all—a good mentor. Developing the habit of thinking first (choosing our words more carefully) is the first step toward improved verbal skills.

> *Wisdom comes in ten parts, nine of which are silence.*
> *The tenth is brevity of language.*
> —SCOTTISH PROVERB

WORDS CAN HEAL

——

IS AN ORGANIZATION DEDICATED TO
HELPING US CHOOSE KINDER WORDS

IT ASKS PEOPLE TO TAKE
THE FOLLOWING PLEDGE:

I pledge to think more about the words I use.

I will try to see how gossip hurts people, including myself, and work to eliminate it from my life.

I will try to replace words that hurt with words that encourage, engage and enrich.

I will not become discouraged when I am unable to choose words perfectly, because making the world a better place is hard work.

And I am pledging to do that, one word at a time.

"Words Can Heal asks you to think before you speak. A simple yet powerful goal: be careful about what you say and how you say it."
—GOLDIE HAWN

WWW.WORDSCANHEAL.ORG

PART TWO

THE WIN-WIN REWARDS
OF POSITIVE WORDS

You have it easily in your power to increase the sum total of this world's happiness now. How? By giving a few words of sincere appreciation to someone who is lonely or discouraged. Perhaps you will forget tomorrow the kind words you say today, but the recipient may cherish them over a lifetime.

—DALE CARNEGIE

CHAPTER 6

JOYFUL WORDS CELEBRATE LIFE

The best use anyone can make of any day is to enjoy it—and then spread that joy to others. Let us celebrate today!

—JOHN KREMER

THE HEART OF THIS BOOK

What you've read so far has been a warm-up for the central message of this book. In the introductory pages and in the first five chapters, I've attempted to lay a foundation regarding our understanding of language in general and the ways we use it in particular. It's important to understand something about the origins of language, the influence of words, and the damage our words can cause not only to others but also to ourselves. These have all been covered to fulfill one of my two goals in writing this book: to increase our awareness of the magnitude of language and to remind us to choose our words wisely.

In this and the following ten chapters I hope to achieve the second, and even more important, goal: to encourage the use of words that celebrate and affirm life. We have the opportunity to do just that every time we open our mouths. Fortunately, there's an abundance of good things to say. All we have to do is look around.

ON BEING A "GOOD FINDER"

In Chapter 4, I wrote about how our words come from the overflow of our hearts—what we tend to store in our minds. I suggested that we start each day by choosing to put something positive into our heads. Good words going in at the beginning of the day are likely to have a positive effect on the way we talk for the rest of that day. But there's another thing we can do that will even further influence what we say: *look for the good.*

Every once in a while we all have an epiphany, one of those special moments in which we "see the light." I had one back in the 1970s when I was reading Zig Ziglar's book *See You at the Top*. I had recently heard him speak and was inspired by his energy and his wisdom. I bought his book so I could read more about his positive and practical approach to living. The epiphany came when I got to page 103. At the top of the page I read these words: "The Good Finders." In this section Ziglar writes about a study conducted on one hundred highly successful people. They ranged in age from early twenties to late seventies and they came from a wide variety of backgrounds. As Ziglar writes, "Other traits and characteristics also varied considerably." But they did have one thing in common: They were all "good finders." They looked for the good "in other people—and in every situation," and they always found it.

As much as I was enjoying the book, I stopped reading and thought long and hard about this simple yet profound concept:

look for the good—in other people, and in every situation. A few old
sayings immediately popped into my mind: (1) "Seek and you
shall find," (2) "We always find what we're looking for," and (3)
"What you see is what you get." It occurred to me that at that
stage in life I wasn't much of a "good finder." In fact, I was pretty
much the opposite. Like many other people, I was much better at
finding the bad and the ugly, and then, of course, complaining
about it. As I said earlier, we live in a culture of complaint. Without even realizing it, we first get infected and then we become
carriers—moaning, whining, grumbling, complaining. We find
the bad and pass it on.

It was at about this same time that a friend had given me my
first Bible. I loved the richness of the literature, the wisdom, the
life-affirming message, and the practical advice it had. And just a
couple days after reading Ziglar's advice to be a "good finder," I
had read the following in one of St. Paul's letters:

> . . . *Fix your minds on whatever is true and honorable*
> *and just and pure and lovely and praiseworthy.*
> —PHILIPPIANS 4:8

That sounds a lot like being a "good finder" to me. And regardless
of what you believe or don't believe spiritually, this is just flat-out,
down-to-earth, practical, day-to-day, commonsense advice—
some of the best you'll ever receive. Look for the good instead of
the bad, the right instead of the wrong, the beauty instead of the
blight, the joy instead of the sorrow. Do this, and you'll always
have something good to say.

After a long period of reflection on Ziglar's and St. Paul's
advice, along with some intense writing in my journal, I resolved
to become a better "good finder." It not only changed my worldview, it changed my attitude, and it changed the way I talk. I can't
say I haven't done any grumbling or complaining since that day,

but I *can* say that I've done a lot less of it. Why waste your time and energy looking for the negative, finding it, and then bringing other people down by talking about it all the time? Doesn't it make a lot more sense to look for the good, find the good, and then celebrate it with others?

Good News

> *Every day that we wake up is a good day. Every breath that we take is filled with hope for a better day. Every word that we speak is a chance to change what is bad into something good.*
>
> —Walter Mosley

Even the news media can find the good. That is, when they look for it. A few years ago, *Newsweek* devoted an entire issue to "Everyday Heroes." In the lead-in for the cover story, the editor in chief wrote that instead of devoting the cover to "wars, crime, and political gridlock," they decided to do one on "some good news." They began looking for ordinary people who had helped others in their communities or performed some act of heroism. Guess what? *Newsweek* found these kinds of people almost everywhere they went. They *looked* for the good—and they *found* the good.

The editor went on to say, " . . . we discovered something very heartening: even in this so-called age of cynicism, ordinary people can make a huge difference." Note that the editor used the phrase "we discovered." The dictionary tells us that "discover" means "to obtain sight or knowledge of for the first time." In other words, the people at *Newsweek* never realized before that there were good people out there doing good things day in and day out. I have to assume that the people who work for this outstanding news-magazine are both bright and dedicated. How is it that they'd been missing all the goodness? Easy answer: They weren't looking for it. Is it any wonder that we get so much bad news from the media? That's what they look for. That's what they find. That's what they report on day after day. That's what fills our heads. And that's what we talk about.

Wouldn't it be nice if the media balanced things up a bit more often? Wouldn't it be nice to be reminded that there are thousands of wonderful people out there doing good things? It would reaffirm our faith in human nature, and it would give us something better to talk about. Instead of devoting just one issue per year to the "quiet heroes and their small victories," maybe *Newsweek* and other news sources could devote at least a section to this type of life-affirming news.

Reading these articles in that special issue was not only uplifting but also inspiring. I remember thinking at the time, "Why don't they do more of this? Why doesn't every newscast, news-magazine, and newspaper give us more things to cheer about? Maybe that's why so many people enjoy reading the sports and entertainment pages. It's easier to find something good. Several years ago, Earl Warren, the Chief Justice of the U.S. Supreme Court in the 1950s and 1960s, said that we read the main section of a newspaper to learn about people's failures, and we read the sports page to learn about their accomplishments.

We all hear people talk about sports. In fact, many women believe that that's all some men *can* talk about. Whether it's true or not, most conversation about sports is positive. Yes, there are complaints about the missed free throw, the error, the dropped pass, and the bonehead decision of the coach, but for the most part, sports talk is animated, lively, and fun. Mainly because when we read the sports page or watch Sports Center on ESPN, we *do* learn of people's accomplishments. It gives us something to celebrate and to share with others. In the news section we get the lowlights of the day; in the sports section we get the highlights. Which would you rather talk about? Which would you rather hear? Whether the media reports on it or not, there's good news all around us. We need to look for it, find it, and share it with others.

WHAT ARE WE CELEBRATING TODAY?

I asked the above question at the beginning of every one of my classes, whether I was teaching kids or adults. Sometimes I asked it a little differently, as in, "Who has good news?" or "Who has something good to say?" However I worded it, it always meant the same thing. It was a call for celebrating life, for focusing on what's right and what's good. And it was always fun! It was part of a life-affirming ritual that started by accident in the 1970–71 school year and continued until I stopped classroom teaching in 2001—thirty years of celebrating! By a conservative estimate, I asked one of these questions at the beginning of class about twenty-seven thousand times. And every time I asked, I got five or more positive responses. That's a lot of celebrating!

Believe it or not, this little ritual started as the result of two things that usually have a negative connotation, especially with kids: current events and homework. At the high school level I often taught courses in United States history and in American government. Whenever I taught either of these two subjects, there was a nightly homework assignment in current events. The average high school kid is woefully uninformed about anything unrelated to music, sports, and other forms of entertainment, so reading the actual news section of a newspaper was a completely new experience for most of them.

Within a few weeks they got the hang of it and were actually surprised at their newly developed ability to carry on an intelligent conversation about what was going on in a world they hardly knew existed just a short time before. Just as we were settling into our routine, a student's innocent observation jolted me. He said, "You know, Dr. Urban, for being such a positive guy, you sure give a negative homework assignment." Somewhat startled, I replied with, "What do you mean?" He simply stated that most of the news was bad news, and he added, "It's kind of a downer." He had me.

We had a long class discussion about this, and I was surprised at how involved the students were. While we had several theories on the reasons for so much bad news, we all agreed on one thing: We needed to receive more good news. This is something I mulled over for quite some time. I was requiring my students to read all this bad news and at the same time jeopardizing my reputation with many of them as "Mr. Positive."

I was now more determined than ever to prove to my students that there was something to celebrate every day and to work a daily dose of good news into our learning environment. So the next day at the beginning of class I asked, "What are we celebrating today?" They thought I meant that it was some day of historical significance, and they should know it. So I said, "Let me ask it a different way: Who has good news? Who has something good to say?" Since this was the first time I'd started class that way, they were a bit mystified. I said, "Since you're having such a hard time finding good news in the newspaper, let's see if we can find some in our own lives." They thought it was a great way to start class, and it developed into something that had a profound and lasting impact on both my students and me.

Over the years of doing this, we heard just about every bit of good news possible. Some were small things, some were huge things. But most important was that my students learned to look for the good in everyday life and then to share it with others. This simple little ritual also had a buildup effect. Each day we added to the good news of the previous day, and so on. And each day my students increased their awareness of all the good news going on around them all the time. They looked for it, they found it, and they celebrated it by sharing it with others.

Over the years I added three more choices as ways to celebrate the day. My students could share something or someone they were thankful for. We called this "perpetual good news." Another option was to say something complimentary about a classmate, and the last one was to share something funny—as long as it was clean. I'll discuss each of these additional ways to celebrate in chapters to follow. They have implications for all of us—at school, within our families, in the workplace, among friends, everywhere.

Since this little ritual of celebration was so popular with my high school students, I thought I'd try it with my adults at the university. My fears that they might be too hardened by life and cynical were quickly allayed. They absolutely loved it and had even more good news than the kids did. Several of these people were in management positions, and they said they liked the idea so much that they'd started opening their regular meetings in much the same way. Their employees also loved it.

As enjoyable as it was to hear good news at least five times a day, I originally had no idea that it would have such a lasting impact on all of us. At the end of that first year of celebrating at the beginning of every class, I received some surprising and valuable feedback on my final exams. Part One of the test was a comprehensive review on all the subject matter covered during the semester and was done in class. Part Two was a take-home exam and allowed the students to express themselves more fully about their learning experiences. These were the instructions: "What are the three things you learned in this class that were of the most value to you? Why? Write one page on each topic."

I was astounded at what I read. Almost every student wrote something about "the way we started class each day." While they did learn valuable things about our history and our government, they felt that sharing good news at the beginning of every class taught them something even more valuable: to look for the good and to celebrate it with others. In my last year of teaching, 2000–01, I ran into a former student I'd taught more than twenty years prior. One of the first things she asked was, "Do you still start class by sharing good news?" After telling her that I couldn't imagine *not* starting class that way, she said, "That was such a great way to start learning. I was glad I was in your first period, because it usually put me in a good mood for the rest of the day. But what it really taught us was to focus on the positive in life instead of the negative. I got in the habit of doing that, so now I always have something good to talk about." Over the years I've heard and read countless similar comments from former students. This small bit of "good finding" for a few minutes each day had an enormous and everlasting influence on many lives, including my own.

> *I cannot help believing that the world would be a bet-*
> *ter and happier place if we'd learn to talk more about*
> *what's right than about what's wrong. We have so much*
> *to celebrate!*
>
> —MICHAEL R. PARRY

Have you heard any good news
Today, today?
I want to hear what you have to say
Wait 'til you get to the count of three
And tell me all the good news
You have for me

One-two-three!

Well now that's really good news
I'm happy to say
It's good, good news today.

—WONDERAMA

CHAPTER 7

AFFIRMING WORDS INSPIRE OTHERS . . . AND OURSELVES

We have experienced how wonderful it feels to receive praise and gratitude from others. It is equally wonderful to give praise.

—SIR JOHN TEMPLETON

ON BEING A LIFE ENHANCER

One of my favorite people is Paula Conlon, who lives right around the corner from our home. She's one of those rare persons who, no matter what your mood is (even if you're already feeling great), can make you feel better. She always shares some bit of good news, extends a compliment or two, asks about me and my family, and laughs uproariously when I make an attempt at humor. How could anyone *not* feel good around her?

A few years ago I attended a birthday party in her honor. At one point during the festivities, Paula was asked to sit in the middle of the room for the traditional birthday song and presentation of gifts. Then the host asked the guests if they would like to say anything about her. Paula was paid some beautiful and well-deserved tributes that day. I can't remember all the nice things that were said about her, but one is etched in my mind forever. Her brother-in-law described her as a "life enhancer." It was the first time I'd ever heard that phrase, and it was the perfect description of Paula.

Merriam-Webster's tells us that to enhance is to *raise* (as in the way Paula raises the spirits of others) or to *improve* (as in the way she improves the quality of life around her). How does she do it? Mostly with kind and affirming words. She always has something good to say.

Driving home that day I thought about another life enhancer who had profoundly changed my life for the better some years earlier. I was in the early stages of my teaching career, was passionate about it, and was working as hard as I could. But somehow, I just didn't feel I was making that special contribution to society that my profession called for. One of the reasons was that I heard from my superiors only when I did something wrong—which seemed often. Naturally, I made matters worse by enlarging their criticism in my head and by becoming my own worst critic.

Then along came Tim Hansel, a teacher who joined our faculty and the social studies department I was in. He was immensely popular with his students and was equally respected by them. I figured I could learn something of value by picking his brain and by watching him teach and interact with the kids. I was right, but didn't know that what I was about to learn would be life changing.

Tim seemed to have a special talent for bringing out the best in people. With his students, instead of focusing on mistakes, he emphasized either what they did right or what they *could* do. He greeted them enthusiastically, praised them for their achievements, and constantly encouraged them to see the opportunities in life and to "go for the good." He did the same with me. He pointed out all the things I was doing right. He said he admired me for my dedication, praised me for my teaching skills, and reminded me how much my students appreciated me. It came at a time when I was in need of some positive feedback. Tim gave me what I wasn't getting from my superiors. It helped me become a better teacher and taught me a great lesson about the power of language. How did Tim do this? The same way Paula did—with kind and affirming words. And like her, he always found something good to say.

Paula and Tim have developed and mastered one of the most powerful human relations skills ever: affirming life in other people. As I wrote in *Life's Greatest Lessons,* I think "affirm" is one of the greatest words in our language. It means looking for, and finding, the good in people and then telling them what you found. It means building others up and encouraging them. It means finding reasons for praise and applause. It means nurturing and being supportive. It means reinforcing what others do well. Most important, it means giving people reasons to celebrate life.

Richard DeVos, the full-of-life founder of the Amway Corporation, wrote eloquently on this topic several years ago. And although I used it in my previous book, I think it's worth repeating. It's one of my all-time favorite quotes:

> *Few things in the world are more powerful than a positive push. A smile. A word of optimism and hope. A "you can do it" when things are tough.*

I love his phrase "positive push." And I agree that there are few things in life with more power for good. When we do something well and are acknowledged for it, we're stimulated to do even better the next time. Sincere praise brings out the best in us. The sad thing is that not enough people realize how much good can be accomplished when they affirm others. Instead of positive pushes, we get negative shoves because we live in a society that seems determined to focus on what's wrong instead of what's right.

More than sixty years ago, Dale Carnegie wrote, "Any fool can criticize, condemn and complain—and most fools do." It's sad that his statement still rings true today. We get bombarded daily with negatives from a variety of sources, and we can't help being influenced by them. But I'm both an optimist and a teacher, and believe deeply that we can change our habits and patterns of speech—if we *want* to. We can train ourselves to look for the good in others and to find reasons for praising them. We can bring about one of those wonderful situations in which everybody wins. Because it's impossible to make another person feel good without doing the same to ourselves. And there are so many ways to do it.

THE THOUGHTFUL THIRTY

Back in Chapter 3 I wrote about the Dirty Thirty—some of the principal ways we can hurt, offend, and drag other people down with our language. Please keep in mind that in the chapter before that I pointed out something we often forget: Our words are choices. We're just as free to choose positive and life-affirming things to say. In fact, there are probably more ways to make other people feel good than there are to offend them.

To test my theory, I used to ask both my teenage and adult students, teachers in my workshops, people on airplanes, and friends the following question: "What are the types of things we can say that make other people—and ourselves—feel good?" Over the years they came up with what became known as the "Thoughtful Thirty." They picked up a few other nicknames along the way. Two of the better ones were "Cheerful Choices" and "Wonder-Working Words." But most of the people I surveyed preferred the idea that these were thoughtful things to say. Here are what they considered to be the best choices for using words to affirm life in others and in ourselves:

1. Give encouragement.
2. Express thanks.
3. Acknowledge others.
4. Extend greetings.
5. Give a compliment.
6. Congratulate someone.
7. Teach, give instructions.
8. Offer words of comfort.
9. Inspire others.
10. Celebrate and cheer.
11. Inquire, express interest.
12. Mend relationships.
13. Make others laugh.
14. Show faith and trust.
15. Share good news.
16. Praise, honor, build up.
17. Express caring.
18. Show understanding and empathy.
19. Give approval.
20. Extend an invitation.
21. Show courtesy and respect.
22. Give advice and counsel.
23. Apologize.
24. Forgive.
25. Offer to help.
26. Tell the truth.
27. Point out the good.
28. Use terms of affection.
29. Provide valuable information.
30. Communicate love.

OUR DEEPEST URGE

The deepest urge in human nature is the desire to feel important.

—JOHN DEWEY

It was in the early 1970s that I first became aware of how powerful affirming words could be. It was then that Tim Hansel came into my life. Tim always left a trail of good feelings behind, everywhere he went. His words filled a basic human need—he made people feel important. He made them feel that their lives mattered. It was fascinating to be around him, and I wanted to learn more about what appeared to be a very special talent.

I needed to improve my own language and human relations skills, and I had the perfect role model in Tim. I also wanted to teach them to others. So for the past thirty-plus years I've been gathering data on the impact of affirming words through surveys and interviews. I can't claim that the findings are based on rigorous scientific research, but the hundreds of stories I've heard from both kids and adults have confirmed over and over that the right words spoken at the right time can be both powerful and long-lasting.

People had some illuminating things to say about the power of positive words in their lives, and, not surprisingly, many of the Thoughtful Thirty came up several times. Three of them, however, stood out.

1. Inquire, express interest

This is probably the simplest method for affirming other people, yet it's the one most overlooked. It's simple because all it involves is asking questions about another person—getting that person to tell you his or her story. It means asking questions that say, "I want to know more about you. You're important." It's overlooked because we're too often waiting for the other person to ask *us* those same questions, to show interest in *us*. It's called human nature. People like to know that they count, that someone else actually *is* interested in them. And it's amazing what a few simple questions can do.

Carnegie, in his classic book *How to Win Friends and Influence People*, gives us six rules that make for outstanding human relations skills:

1. Become genuinely interested in other people.
2. Smile.
3. Remember that a person's name is to that person the sweetest and most important sound in any language.
4. Be a good listener. Encourage others to talk about themselves.
5. Talk in terms of the other person's interest.
6. Make the other person feel important—and do it sincerely.

You'll note that two of Carnegie's rules are nonverbal: smile and listen—powerful communication skills that enrich any conversation. All the rest focus on finding out more about the person you're talking to. This can be done by asking questions that show you're genuinely interested. Each answer you receive will lead to additional questions, and you'll eventually get the other person to feel that he or she actually does count. Sadly, too many people in our celebrity-worshipping nation feel that they *don't* count, that they're not important. A few good questions can often change that. Carnegie says, "Ask questions that other persons will enjoy answering. Encourage them to talk about themselves and their accomplishments."

A case in point: Princess Marie Louise, Queen Victoria's granddaughter, met several famous and powerful people in England during the 1800s. Two of them were Benjamin Disraeli and

William Gladstone, who both served as prime minister. After being taken to dinner one evening by Gladstone and the following evening by Disraeli, she was asked what impressions these two distinguished statesmen had made on her. She said, "When I left the dining room after sitting next to Mr. Gladstone I thought he was the cleverest man in England. But after sitting next to Mr. Disraeli I thought I was the cleverest woman in England."

2. Give encouragement/inspire others

These are some of the definitions of "encourage" listed in *Merriam-Webster's Dictionary:*

- "to fill with courage or strength of purpose"
- "to inspirit, hearten, embolden"
- "to instill life, energy, courage, or vigor"
- "to infuse with fresh courage or zeal"
- "to give courage sufficient to overcome timidity or reluctance"

To encourage another person is often all of these—and then some. It literally means *to give courage.* The right words spoken at the right time can often be one of the most positive, life-affirming, and long-lasting gifts you'll ever give. Our history books and biographies are full of stories about great men and women who've made marvelous achievements and improved the quality of life for all of us. And if you read those stories, you'll find that most great people were first inspired and encouraged by someone else. You'll find in their backgrounds a parent or other relative, a friend, colleague, teacher, pastor, mentor, coach, or other person who believed in them and communicated it clearly. That's why Richard DeVos says there's nothing more powerful than a "positive push." He probably received a few himself on his way to great success in the business world.

I got hooked on biographies at age twelve, and it proved to be a valuable and enjoyable addiction. It also taught me about the power of encouragement. That first biography was of Thomas Edison, and there's a story in it that I'll never forget. Edison didn't last very long in school. He had what today we would call attention deficit disorder, but there was no name for it then. His teacher did the exact opposite of what she should have done—she pinned a negative and destructive label on him. To make matters worse, she gave it to him in front of other children. She said his brain was "addled," which means confused, and the kids in his school began to call him "Addle." His mother, understanding the damage that negative nicknames can do, took him out of school and educated him at home. And at every step along the way, she encouraged him. She saw his genius, she told him she saw it, and she inspired him to greatness. To the end of his days, Edison praised and thanked his mother for her belief in him and for her encouragement.

This is only one of literally countless stories of encouragement throughout history. If you want to read an entire book about encouraging words, see Marlo Thomas's inspiring and uplifting book *The Right Words at the Right Time*. This gifted actress tells the stories of 110 celebrities who were dramatically influenced by the words of someone else on the way up. Sorry, I don't know any celebrities, but I know hundreds of historical figures and regular people whose lives were changed by the energizing and stimulating words of a friend or relative. They also were given courage by another person.

Thomas says her fascination with the power of encouraging words started when she was only seventeen. She was struggling in the early stages of her acting career when her father said just the right thing to her. It not only changed her life at the time, it had a lasting impact. Those words of her father were what later inspired her to write the book. She concluded that everyone she knew and admired probably had a similar story. She was right.

Writing in *Parade* magazine about her reason for writing the book, she says:

> *Each of us goes through a time when we're at a cross-*
> *road and not sure what to do next. Then someone comes*
> *along and says just the right words to get us through it.*

One of Thomas's main points is that, in addition to getting us through a difficult or critical moment, the right words remain in our hearts and "stay with us for the rest of our lives." Although she had heard the well-known phrase that "actions speak louder than words," she became increasingly aware that words also speak very loudly and that they sometimes last a lifetime. She added, "I've discovered how important it is to turn up the volume on the good words in our heads—to use them, nosh on them, make them a model for ourselves."

3. Praise, honor, build up

Almost every day of our lives is filled with several opportunities to fill that basic need of all people to feel as if they matter. We can give compliments, we can express admiration, we can acknowl-dege hard work, we can tell people how much they're appreciated, we can congratulate them, we can honor them in a myriad of ways. With just a little bit of thoughtfulness, and without being phony, we can give someone the unexpected gift of affirming words. It might have a pleasant effect and last only a short time, and it might have a powerful effect and last forever.

All we need to do is follow Zig Ziglar's advice more often—look for the good—and then take a few minutes to comment on it. One place we're sure to find it is in what people are doing all around us. There are colleagues, students, family members, and other people who help us daily in a variety of ways who would love to receive a little more positive feedback. In fact, too many people are *starving* for it. Here are a couple of simple, yet power-ful, examples of making someone else's day.

The chefs. Maybe you've said or heard another person say to the server at the end of a good meal in a restaurant, "My compli-ments to the chef." Who knows whether the chef actually gets the compliment, and if he or she does, how it's delivered? My friend Carl made sure it was delivered—and in the right way. We were at a conference in St. Louis and had dinner together in an Italian restaurant, where we both ordered seafood pasta. Within only a few minutes we both agreed that it was the most delicious we'd ever tasted.

At the end of the meal, I thanked the waitress for her excellent service and added the usual, "Our compliments to the chef." Carl said, "We can do better than that. Let's go tell him." He then asked for, and received, permission to go into the kitchen. The two chefs looked surprised to see a stranger in their midst. Carl immediately asked, "Which one of you guys made that delicious seafood pasta?" They got big smiles on their faces, and one said proudly, "We both did." "Fantastic!" Carl said. "It's my favorite dinner, and you just cooked up the best one I've ever tasted. Thank you. You've made our evenings." They glowed and thanked him. I think Carl made their evenings also. On the way out he found the restaurant manager and told her the same thing. In less than one minute, Carl left a trail of good feelings and goodwill behind him that is probably still felt today.

The gate agent. I was at the Dayton, Ohio, airport a few years ago on what may have been one of the nastiest nights in aviation history—lightning, thunder showers, delayed flights, canceled flights, and lots of frustrated and angry people. You couldn't pay me enough to be a gate agent on a night like that. Too many inex-perienced travelers have to find someone to take out their frustra-tions on, and that's who gets it. I couldn't help feeling sorry for the agent that evening. He had an angry mob on his hands. I also couldn't help admiring him for the way he was handling it. He stayed calm, was efficient and helpful, and was polite to people who were being incredibly rude and unreasonable to him.

While I was admiring him, someone else actually *said* to him what I was thinking. The man in front of me, after finally getting to the counter, told the agent, "You know, I've been admiring you for almost an hour now, and if I was grading you, I'd give you an A+ in customer service. You've defused an explosive situation, you've calmed down angry people, you've shown respect to those who've disrespected you, and you've provided excellent service with class and dignity. I wish you worked for me." The gate agent, whose name was Rob, beamed and humbly thanked the man. I could tell that this most deserved recognition and praise made his day—maybe his year.

But the man with the affirming words wasn't finished. He then said, "I'd like to have your name and employee number, young man. I think United Airlines should know about what a great job you're doing, and I want to write and tell them." After being yelled at for more than an hour, Rob finally got the kind of recognition he deserved. All because the man looked for the good, found it, and communicated it.

More than a year later, I was in that same airport under more pleasant conditions—perfect weather, no delays, no canceled flights, no angry people. And guess who checked me in? Right, it was Rob. I had to ask him. Did he remember that evening fourteen months earlier? "Do I ever!" he said. "What was my worst night on the job became my best night because of what that man said to me. I'll never forget it as long as I live." He also told me that the man followed through and wrote to United about him. "That made it even more special," Rob said. Those kind words that took a few minutes to speak and to write will probably last a lifetime.

PRAISE IS ALWAYS WIN-WIN

*It could be that we ourselves are the principal benefici-
aries of our praise.*

—ADAIR LARA

In the quote at the beginning of this chapter, Sir John Templeton states that giving praise is "equally wonderful" as receiving it. Maybe that's why the saying "It's better to give than to receive" has been around since biblical times.

On the last page of *Life's Greatest Lessons,* I made a simple statement: "As human beings, we need to be good." It's probably the closest I've ever come to saying something profound. I also stated that there's a direct relationship between being good and living a quality life. One of the best ways we can *be good* is to bring out the best in other people. And we do that every time we give honest and sincere praise. We need to be reminded of the wisdom in that old saying about giving and receiving, even though we're bombarded daily with messages that claim the opposite.

Is it possible not to feel better about ourselves when we know we've made someone else feel good? I don't think it is. That's probably why Stephen Covey says one of the best habits we'll ever have is to look for and create win-win situations with the other people in our lives. Recognition and praise will always do that.

*We increase whatever we praise. The whole creation
responds to praise, and is glad.*

—CHARLES FILLMORE

You cannot receive a sincere compliment without feeling better . . . and just as important, you cannot give a sincere compliment without feeling better yourself.

—Zig Ziglar

CHAPTER 8

LOVING WORDS BUILD AND HEAL RELATIONSHIPS

What others need from us, on an ongoing basis, is to know that they are cared for, that their good deeds inspire gratitude, and that others love them. It's that simple. And just because they hear such sentiments on Monday doesn't mean that they won't need to hear them again on Tuesday. This is the primary reason why words that heal and inspire must be repeated again and again.

—RABBI JOSEPH TELUSHKIN

LOVING WORDS COME FROM FINDING THE GOOD

As indicated in the previous chapter, the seeds of this book were planted many years ago when I met Tim Hansel. I was immediately drawn to him because he was such an "upper." Whether he was talking about something or someone pertaining to the school we were teaching at or about any other facet of life, Tim always let me know that he had found the good and wanted to talk about it.

Tim's positive words had a profound effect on both his students and his colleagues. People wanted to be around him because he brightened their day even if they were already having a good one. He seemed to have developed a special skill for letting people know that they mattered and were appreciated. I couldn't count the number of times he changed the subject in one of our conversations just to let me know how much he liked me. We'd be talking about sports, or school, or books, or faith, or anything. He'd stop right in the middle of the discussion, get a big smile on his face, point at me, and ask, "Do you know what I like most about you?" And before I could answer, he'd proceed to tell me about the good he found in me on that particular day. I can't help thinking that we could enhance many of our relationships by simply letting friends know more often that we're finding the good in them.

We experience the world largely through interacting with others, so our relationships, especially with friends, are at the very core of our existence. The words we use and the words we hear will often determine the quality of these relationships and, in turn, the quality of our lives. Whether these friendships are within the family or outside of it, the words we choose can build and strengthen them and, at times, restore and heal them. While we don't always feel the need to express our love and appreciation for our friends, they probably feel the need to hear it more often. As Rabbi Telushkin reminds us, "It's that simple."

LOVING WORDS NURTURE COUPLES

Many couples have never learned the tremendous power of verbally affirming each other.

—GARY CHAPMAN

Let's define a couple as two people who have made a commitment to one another. This includes people who are seriously dating, engaged, living together, or married. The key in any of these relationships is communication: what the two persons say to each other and how they say it. Since romance is usually the starting point for two people in becoming a couple, we know that both of them were careful to "say the right things" in the early stages.

If each continues to choose words carefully, there's a high probability that the relationship will go from good to better. But as we know, people often slack off on their "sweet talk" once the relationship is established. Psychologists and marriage counselors tell us couples are likely to fall into one or more of four communication traps:

1. They talk less, sometimes unconsciously regarding the other person as a piece of furniture that's just "there."
2. They take each other for granted, often forgetting to acknowledge and/or express thanks.
3. They get mentally lazy. Instead of choosing words that enrich the relationship, they slip into verbal ruts. The loving words that helped build the relationship begin to decrease and eventually disappear.
4. They start using their partner as a verbal dumping ground for complaints, criticism, demands, etc.

While these problems can damage our relationships, the good news is that, with some increased awareness and effort, they can be easily corrected. Family therapists often ask couples about the communication patterns they've developed. Invariably, one or more of the four above come up. Recognizing the problem is the first step toward solving it.

A case in point: A few years ago my wife, Cathy, helped me recognize that I had fallen into one of these traps over the course of our marriage. It's the one that I suspect most of us fall into: mental laziness and an accompanying verbal rut. Partners frequently ask for each other's help. In our case, Cathy often asks me to help her reach something, take out the garbage, or help with the cleaning. I always do what she asks of me, but not without a little grumbling first. It had become a habit, and I was oblivious of her need to have me do these little chores in a better spirit.

One day she asked me nicely to get some plates down for her, and I both grumbled and said that I would do it later. Knowing that I was working on a book about using positive words, she issued me a friendly challenge. In a pleasant tone, she said, "It would be so nice to ask you to do something and someday hear you answer, 'Yes, honey. I'd be happy to do that for you, and I'll do it right away.'"

I'd not only been caught in the act but also challenged to put my positive words into practice. As you might suspect, that's now my standard response to all her requests for help. And even though I ham it up a little with the tone and facial expression, Cathy always gets both a pleasant response and immediate aid. This simple little change in words and tone brings about win-win every time.

The additional good news is that there are other simple ways we can strengthen all of our relationships.

THE FIVE *A*'S OF HEALTHY COMMUNICATION

The deepest principle of human nature is the craving to be appreciated.

          —WILLIAM JAMES

A reminder from an earlier chapter: Words are choices. The more we remember that simple statement, the more likely we are to use words that sustain our important relationships and make our significant others feel as if they count. As the great psychologist William James points out, we all have a "craving" to be valued and treasured.

Here are five practical *A*'s.

- **Attention.** As in paying attention to the other person and his or her needs, and to the opportunities we have to say something kind and uplifting.
- **Appreciation.** As in saying "thank you" more often, even for those things we've grown accustomed to receiving from our loved ones.
- **Ask.** As in asking about activities and plans and hopes and joys and concerns of the other person. And as in asking what we can do to help.
- **Affection.** As in using terms of affection. Has anyone ever complained about being told "I love you" or hearing "You're the best" too many times? Has anyone ever tired of being called "Honey" or "Sweetie" too often by his or her partner?
- **Affirm.** As in acknowledging, building up, and encouraging; as in being a one-person cheering section for this person you care so much about.

LOVING WORDS STRENGTHEN FRIENDSHIPS

*Good friends always let us know that we're special . . .
and why.*

—PATTI STEMPLE

While we usually don't fall into the same communication traps with our friends outside the family, we still need to remind ourselves that they too have a craving to be appreciated. We also need to remind ourselves to not take our friends for granted. Like anyone else, they need some positive feedback from time to time. I've always thought that Tim's question, "Do you know what I like most about you?" was the perfect one for friends to ask each other. On different days we appreciate different qualities about our friends . . . and we need to tell them. We have nothing to lose, we'll make two people feel better, and we'll make a strong relationship even stronger.

"Friend" is one of the most positive and powerful words ever invented, no matter what the language. To be called a friend is to receive high praise, and to call someone else a friend is to give one of the highest compliments possible. And there's yet another simple way that the word "friend" becomes magical—when we use it in place of the person's name in a greeting. I was taught many years ago that people like to hear their own names. So it's better to say, "Hi, Bill," than it is just to say, "Hi." It personalizes the greeting. Better yet is saying, "Hi, Friend." It's a simple way of saying, "You're special to me," and people love hearing it.

Here are a few more examples of using affectionate words to enrich a relationship:

- Cathy and her best friend, Sylvia, greet each other, both over the phone and in person, with, "Hello, Girlfriend." Here are two women past the age of fifty using a term of endearment to remind each other how valued each other is and how treasured their relationship is.

- I had two male students a few years ago who addressed each other as "Best Friend." It was their way of telling each other and everyone around them how strongly they felt about each other.

- One of my students used to greet me every day in the same manner: "Hello, Favorite Teacher." Even though I heard this greeting over and over, I never once got tired of it. In fact, whether it was the first day of the year or the last day, she made me feel good every time she said it.

- My friend Tim had a lot of friendly nicknames for his students when we taught together in the early 1970s. They loved them. They were simple terms that always described the student in a positive way. A few that I remember were "Muscles" (best used on a male who's into weight lifting), "Handsome," "Gorgeous," "Giggles," "Happy Face," "Einstein." He often greeted people with "Hello, Human Being," and because we so often get treated as if we're objects, it always had a special ring to it.

- While I was writing this book, I received an e-mail that had two words in the subject line: "Thanks, Friend." I had recently done a small favor for a person I greatly admire, so I lit up when I saw it. This is a great example of the power that positive words can have. In a matter of seconds, he made me feel appreciated for what I had done and reminded me of the bond between us.

LOVING WORDS HEAL RELATIONSHIPS

The tongue that brings healing is a tree of life.
—PROVERBS 15:4

The two phrases that have the most power to heal a damaged relationship just happen to also be the two phrases that are the hardest for us to say:

* * *

"I was wrong."

"I'm sorry."

They're the hardest to say because most of us never want to admit that we caused a breach in the relationship. It was the other person's fault, and we're waiting for him or her to apologize. But the apology never comes because the other person is also waiting for it. And as we know, close relationships, both within the family and outside of it, sometimes end permanently for lack of this apology.

Why is it so hard to admit that we were wrong and to apologize? The answer is human nature. We're born with some innate weaknesses, and one of the big ones is devotion to self. Overcoming it signifies personal growth, empathy, and caring—exactly what we need to heal our important relationships. A simple apology can work wonders.

What do you do when you want to restore the relationship, but you really don't think you did anything wrong? First, keep in mind that the other person feels the same way. What's important is to say something that can lead to healing. Example: "I'm really sorry we're having this problem. Can we talk about making things right?" Taking a step like this almost always leads to healing. And in most cases, the conversation results in both people apologizing. It also usually results in an even stronger relationship.

Any kind of healing in a relationship obviously involves some degree of forgiveness, something that must come from the heart before it's stated in words. Expressing it comes with a caution, however. "I forgive you" in the middle of a squabble might come across as, "You were wrong," and make things even worse. We should say, "I forgive you," only when someone asks to be forgiven. Then they're the perfect words. Forgiveness has the power to heal not only the relationship but also the bodies and the minds of both people.

Among people of the Jewish faith, the holiest day of the year is Yom Kippur, the Day of Atonement. It's a day set aside for prayer and fasting while people account for their sins and seek reconciliation with God. According to tradition, a person who sincerely repents on this day will be forgiven by God. But there's another part to this great day of healing. It involves being forgiven by those who have been offended. This can't happen until the offending person goes to the one who was hurt and speaks healing words. Wouldn't it be nice if there was a National Day of Atonement, regardless of faith, in which we were asked to try to heal our broken relationships? Better yet, we can make any day we want to be one of atonement. We already have the words. We just need to say them.

LOVING WORDS OFFER COMFORT

While loving words can mend and heal our relationships, they can also comfort people who are going through hard times. I'm referring to things like the death of a loved one, a serious illness or injury, the loss of a job, the end of a romance, or some other misfortune beyond their control. The biggest mistake we can make when these things happen is to say nothing. People often do this for one reason: They don't know what to say. Admittedly, it's hard to come up with just the right words for every occasion, but it's always better to try than to say nothing. Silence can easily be interpreted as not caring.

This difficulty came up often when I was teaching courses in communication to both high school kids and to adults at the university. I frequently heard comments like these: "It's so awkward," "I didn't know what to say," "I was afraid I would say the wrong thing," "I was too embarrassed."

My advice was always the same: Say something that comes from the heart. Even if you have to begin your comments with "I wish I had the perfect words of comfort for you right now . . . ," whatever you say will be appreciated, as long as it's sincere. "Tell me how I can help" is good in almost any situation. No matter how awkward or embarrassing it is, say it in the best way you can. Your words must be spoken or written before they can be comforting.

There's one common mistake people make when trying to comfort others. They say, "I know how you feel," when, in fact, they don't. Example: If a friend's father dies or a friend gets cancer, don't say "I know how you feel" unless your own father has died or you've had cancer yourself. In those cases you can be of great comfort, but if you haven't experienced what your friend is going through, your remarks will come across as insincere. The key is to think first and then say the most comforting thing you can. If your heart's in the right place, you'll come up with the right words.

Gentle speech makes friends.
                                        —WISDOM OF SIRACH

Be slow to anger, slow to blame,
And slow to plead thy cause.
But swift to speak of any gain
That gives thy friend applause.

—MARY WHITCHER

CHAPTER 9

GRACIOUS WORDS
SHOW RESPECT
AND GRATITUDE

Throughout the United States, people seem to feel that the phrase "common courtesy" has become a contradiction in terms.

—THE WALL STREET JOURNAL

WHATEVER HAPPENED TO GOOD MANNERS?

One of the Flagrant Four listed in Chapter 3 was "rude and inconsiderate language." It seems that for the past several years we've been having a crisis in civility. Some people regard it as a minor ailment while others see it as an epidemic. But almost everyone agrees that it's a problem. When I give talks about language, whether it's to student groups, educators, parents, or people in business, I begin by asking a question: "Which of the following types of language better represent the kind of environment you want to live in?" Using either signs or overheads, I show them the first one:

Language that is . . .

civil
respectful
courteous
kind
considerate
polite
gentle

Then I show them the second one:

Language that is . . .

rude
crude
raw
coarse
filthy
angry
mean

It's no surprise that the overwhelming majority of people in those audiences say that the first sign better describes the type of language they'd most like to hear. But then I ask four more questions. The first one is, "How many of you hear the type of language indicated on the second sign?" All the hands go up. Then the next question: "How many of you think you hear *too much* of the second type of language?" Almost all of the hands go up. Then, the third question: "How many of you *use* the second type of language?" A few hands go up in adult audiences; quite a few go up in student audiences. And finally, "How many of you are free to choose the type of language that comes out of your mouth?" After a bit of hesitation—because they have to think about it for a moment—all the hands go up again.

If the first type of language is better and if we're all free to choose it rather than the second type, then why are we having a problem? There are several theories, and they're probably all correct. One is that the entertainment industry not only bombards us with foul and mean language but also glorifies it. It's cool when famous athletes, movie stars, and musicians use it. Another is that more and more people are stressed, in a hurry, frustrated, and angry, thus more likely to express themselves with harsh language. Another is that it's part of a steady deterioration of our culture. Standards have been sinking lower each year since the late 1960s.

A few years ago *U.S. News & World Report* ran a cover story titled "In Your Face." The subtitle asked this question: "Whatever Happened to Good Manners?" The article itself was headlined "The American Uncivil Wars" and had this subheadline: "How crude, rude and obnoxious behavior has replaced good manners and why that hurts our politics and culture." Among the results of a poll conducted by Bozell Worldwide are these:

- Nine out of ten Americans think incivility is a problem.
- More than half of them think it is a serious problem.
- Seventy-eight percent say the problem has worsened in the last ten years.
- More than ninety percent believe it contributes to an increase in violence.

- Eighty-five percent believe it divides the national community.
- Eighty-five percent see it eroding healthy values like respect for others.
- Seventy-three percent say mean-spirited political campaigns are a cause of people being less civil.
- Ninety-nine percent of Americans say that their own behavior is civil.

IS THERE A SOLUTION? YES

Almost everyone agrees that the increasing use of rude language is a problem. But instead of trying to pinpoint the theory that best explains it, or measuring the magnitude of the problem, or finding out who's to blame, or determining where it's leading us, we should be doing something far more important: looking for a solution. Is there one? As I said on the first page of the first chapter, I have a positive worldview, and I'm optimistic enough, along with a lot of other people, to believe that we can go a long way toward restoring civility and polite language to our society.

I learned a valuable lesson in problem solving early in my career. During my first year of teaching, I complained to the principal about something that was wrong at the school. It must not have been too important, because I don't remember what it was. But I *do* remember the response from the principal—and won't ever forget it. In a nice way, he said, "I agree that it's a problem. Which do you want to be—part of the problem or part of the solution?" He had me. We had a great talk, got others involved, and actually solved the problem. Complaining about the problem didn't help. Looking for a solution did.

A few years later I read something in Scott Peck's classic book, *The Road Less Traveled,* that reminded me of the problem or solution choice. It also stuck with me. He states, "Life is a series of problems. Do we want to moan about them or solve them?" Peck goes on to say, "Problems call forth our courage and our wisdom; indeed, they create our courage and wisdom."

It takes neither courage nor wisdom to complain. Every time I hear people moan and groan about how our society is deteriorating, I want to ask them the same question my principal asked me or the same one Peck asks in his book. I wonder if it ever occurred to them that their moaning and groaning actually make the problem worse.

SUGGESTIONS FROM A FEW EXPERTS

He who sows courtesy, reaps friendship, and he who plants kindness, gathers love.

—NEEDLES AND FRIENDS

Judith Martin is one of our foremost authorities on courtesy. In fact, she's so well-known that many people don't know her real name. That's because she writes under another name that's far more recognizable: Miss Manners. Her column appears weekly in papers throughout the country, and she has a well-earned reputation for having both wisdom and common sense, and for giving sound advice when it comes to social mores.

Miss Manners sees some positive signs in the fact that so many people are keenly aware of the problem. It has to be recognized before it can be solved. She says, "I see some hope because the problem has been identified." She also points out that we've just about bottomed out, so we have no place to go but up. Martin sees awareness as the first step toward improving our social discourse. If enough individuals and institutions see the problem and the solution, we can at least move upward.

Letitia Baldrige was called "America's leading arbiter of manners" by *Time* magazine. She's served in the American embassies in both Paris and Rome, and was Jacqueline Kennedy's chief of staff in the White House. She's written books on manners, business conduct, and human behavior. Baldridge also sees hope. She says people rarely use offensive language with the actual intent of *being* offensive. They use it out of habit and because it's become so commonplace. She suggests we need to do a better job at home and in schools to help young people get started in the right direction regarding manners and language. She also believes we can make a difference.

Psychiatrist Scott Peck and sociologist Amitai Etzioni both believe that if we place greater emphasis on civility and kind words in our institutions and communities, we'll create a more nourishing environment. In *A World Waiting to Be Born: Civility Rediscovered*, Peck writes that we need to "resurrect and redefine the meaning of civility. This is necessary for the healing of our society." He says our institutions need to do a better job of reminding people about the almost forgotten glory of simply being human. Etzioni, in his book *The New Golden Rule*, says we need to stretch ourselves beyond preoccupation with self and think more about the community and the society in which we live. While he respects the legal right of free speech, he also believes that members of the community are fully entitled to inform those who "spout venom" that their language is offensive. We *can* make a difference within our institutions and our communities.

LET'S GO BACK TO THE BASICS, STARTING WITH THE MAGIC WORDS

We're talking 'bout please and thank you,
They're called the magic words.
If you want nice things to happen,
They're the words that should be heard!
—PHIL PARKER

I was standing in the line at the post office recently and witnessed the following. When the man in front of me approached the window, the postal clerk greeted him politely and asked, "How may I help you, sir?" The answer, in a rather aggressive manner and tone, was, "I need a roll of stamps." The clerk handed him the stamps and asked, "Is there anything else I can do for you?" In the same tone and manner, he said, "Yeah, gimme a couple of those Priority Mail envelopes." She did so with a smile. He took the stamps and the envelopes and paid her in cash. She handed him a receipt and said, "Thank you very much." He turned and walked away.

Sadly, we're experiencing more and more of these types of incidents in our daily lives. They're not horrendous, they're just rude, and they're happening with alarming frequency. This is only one of several examples I could have selected from the past few days. I chose this one because it was so typical of what we see and hear— and what we *don't* hear. "Please" and "thank you" are still in the dictionary, but many of us wonder if they're disappearing from our daily discourse.

During the first twenty years of my teaching career, those two pillars of courtesy were automatic. If a student needed something from me, the request always began with the magic words "May I please have . . ." asked in a pleasant tone. Upon receiving the desired object, the student said just as automatically and politely, "Thank you very much." Times have changed. Sometime during the mid-1980s, "May I please have" in a pleasant tone turned into "I need" in a demanding tone. And "Thank you" in a pleasant tone turned into nothing.

Then I started hearing "I need" and "gimme" (like the guy at the post office) much more frequently among people of all ages. Is it any wonder that our kids have some shortcomings in the manners department? But let's not blame them. Kids will always be a reflection of what's going on in the adult world.

Around 1987 I decided to be proactive about manners, with an emphasis on language, at the beginning of the school year. This was with both my high school and my university students. Most of the latter were in a professional degree program and were in their thirties and forties. I was more than a little concerned that my students at both levels might regard me as an old fogey who couldn't keep pace and wanted to return to the good old days. How I approached them on the subject was critical.

I asked them if the atmosphere in the classroom was important to them. It was. I asked them if they knew what the Golden Rule was. A few did, many didn't. I just happened to have copies of fourteen versions of it with me. These were from a wide variety of philosophers, religious leaders, and political figures throughout history. In essence, they all said the same thing: Treat other people the way you'd like them to treat you. Then I asked them if they knew what win-win was. Most of the adults knew, many of the kids didn't, but they figured it out in a hurry. I asked them, "If we all apply the Golden Rule in the classroom, will it result in win-win." They all agreed that it would.

We had a great discussion about manners and language, and how both had been deteriorating, even in classrooms. I asked all of them to share stories about when they first learned about the magic words. Not surprisingly, they had vivid memories and interesting anecdotes. And everyone agreed that the magic words and other forms of common courtesy need to be brought back. When I did this the first time, I was surprised at how many students thanked me. One of my high school seniors said, "We know these things, but sometimes we need to be reminded about how important they are."

*   *   *

If It Worked in New York, It Can Work Anywhere

People do talk about a time in America when there was more respect and civility. How do we return to that kinder, gentler world? It will take both a significant individual and collective resolve to cure what has become an epidemic.

—Deborah Wadsworth

When I visited New York City for the first time in the early 1970s, I thought it was the most exciting place I'd ever been. There was something absolutely electric about it. There was, however, a downside. New York was also the rudest place I'd ever been. It seemed as if everybody who lived or worked there had an edge, and the language was the worst I'd ever heard outside of a Joe Pesci movie. The cab drivers, of course, were notorious, but they weren't the only ones with foul mouths. I got the impression, as did many other visitors, that most of the people in New York were either angry, rude, or both.

The dirty streets and the dirty language appeared to be part of a package deal. You couldn't have the excitement without the filth. "It's part of our charm," one New Yorker told me. He also said that if you were going to live or visit there, you'd just have to put up with it: "It's been this way for a long time, and it ain't ever gonna change." I figured his assessment was accurate, so I learned to accept the bad along with the good over the next sixteen years while making my annual pilgrimage to this great city.

But it turned out that his assessment *wasn't* accurate. The social climate of New York *did* change—and it changed dramatically. It changed because one man believed that New York City could be a cleaner and nicer place to visit, live in, and work in. That man was Rudy Giuliani, who became the mayor in 1994.

When he said New York was going to shed its image as a dirty and rude city, residents, workers, visitors, and the media scoffed. Some thought the term "polite New Yorker" was an oxymoron, some laughed, and some said sarcastically, "Yeah, right!"

But New York did become a cleaner and more polite city because Giuliani believed it could, and he was able to convince others that it would be a win-win situation for everyone. When Cathy and I visited New York in the spring of 2001, we hadn't been there for about ten years. We were astounded at what we saw and what we heard—and what we *didn't* hear. Even the cab drivers were polite! It *can* be done.

Maybe Rudy Giuliani or someone like him is the "significant individual" referred to in the quote at the beginning of this section. We could use a respected national figure to get us back on the right track. But "collective resolve" is also part of the quote. We need that, too.

AGENTS OF CHANGE

> *Our levels of political, social, and commercial discourse are now so low that it is surely time to try restoring civility from the bottom up.*
>
> —JOHN LEO

Some of the most uncivil language we hear comes from the people we elected to represent us in our state and federal governments. They spend more time verbally tearing each other apart than they do talking about what they're doing for the good of the country. We can't expect them to take the lead in restoring civil and polite language to our culture. There are, however, some mainstream institutions that can make a real difference if the people in them believe they can—and want to. I'm referring specifically to families, schools, businesses, and local governments.

Families and schools

Thousands of families and schools have been forming win-win partnerships since the early 1990s under the umbrella of Character Education. The progress has been phenomenal, and these partnerships continue to grow as more and more schools develop programs. What is Character Education? It's a commitment by the people who work in a school to achieve a dual goal: teach academic subjects while helping young people develop the solid character traits that help them become good citizens—ones who are kind and considerate of others and whose language is clean and life affirming. A primary aim is to turn the school into a "caring community," one in which teachers are able to teach and students are able to learn in a safe and supportive atmosphere.

Let me share with you just one of many examples of how an effective schoolwide Character Education program influences good manners and polite language. In 2002, I spoke at Glenbard North High School in the Chicago suburb of Carol Stream, Illinois. It's a public school with more than twenty-eight hundred kids. What kind of manners and language do you envision in a setting with twenty-eight hundred teenagers? I've asked that question to many people since visiting the school. I usually get one-word answers like "rude," "crude," "dirty," "gross," etc.

But that was not the case. The kids were dressed well and their manners were flawless. And I did not hear a single rude or dirty word during my entire day on the campus. This is the result when families and schools work together in bringing out the best in kids and in promoting appropriate language. It happened in this school because the staff believed it could and worked to make it happen. My visit there was an experience I'll never forget.

*   *   *

Businesses and local governments

Never underestimate the power of leadership in a community to bring about positive change—including the restoration of civility and polite language. If Rudy Giuliani could bring it about in New York City, think what leaders could do in smaller cities. It takes only a small number of committed people to get the ball rolling. In fact, that's how all major changes begin. And as others begin to see the benefits, they'll not only buy in but also become contributors. When businesses, local governments, service organizations like the Rotary, Lions, and Chamber of Commerce, and places of worship join hands, they can create a "caring community"—not just to go to school in but also to *live* in.

This is actually happening in some of our cities. One of the best examples is Chattanooga, Tennessee, a city of about 150,000 people. The Character Education program that had begun in the public schools of Chattanooga eventually became a citywide program. City leaders not only bought into it but also became enthusiastic about it. Among other things, you see huge billboards in various locations throughout the city promoting courtesy and respect. The people who live in Chattanooga are justly proud of the culture they've created there in recent years. They're also proud of the several national awards for "outstanding livability" their city has won.

Whether it's New York or Chattanooga, a college or high school classroom, a school or community, the bottom line is that it *can* be done.

A kind mouth multiplies friends and appeases enemies,
and gracious lips prompt friendly greetings.
                                        —WISDOM OF SIRACH

King Solomon on Words of Respect

The mouth of the righteous is a fountain of life. 10:11

He who guards his lips guards his life. . . . 13:3

The lips of the wise spread knowledge. . . . 15:7

Pleasant words are a honeycomb, sweet to the soul and healing to the bones. 16:24

A word aptly spoken is like apples of gold in settings of silver. 25:11

FROM THE BOOK OF PROVERBS

Chapter 10

Funny Words
Make Us Laugh

When people are laughing, they're generally not killing one another.

—Alan Alda

I am thankful for laughter, except when milk comes out of my nose.

—Woody Allen

The Healthy Effects of Laughter

Before I wrote a chapter about humor in my first book, I did a lot of reading about the benefits of laughter. The old saying that "laughter is good medicine" was being proved true by medical researchers. One of the pioneers in the field was Norman Cousins, a well-known literary figure who used laughter and positive thinking to cure himself of a deadly disease. He wrote about it in 1979 in *Anatomy of an Illness,* a book that became a best seller and is still widely read. Cousins went on to become the first person without an M.D. to teach medicine. He taught at the UCLA Medical School, where he established the Humor Task Force, and continued to do research and write about the healthy effects of laughter. Since his groundbreaking work, many in the medical profession have not only proved but also strengthened his theories. Here's a summary of recent findings:

Therapeutic Benefits of Laughter

- It activates and strengthens the immune system.
- It reduces at least four hormones associated with stress.
- It's aerobic. It provides a "workout" for the diaphragm and increases the body's ability to use oxygen.
- It relaxes the muscles.
- It can significantly reduce pain for long periods.
- It lowers blood pressure and can prevent hypertension.
- It improves respiration by emptying the lungs completely of the air they take in.
- It has no negative side effects.
- It's available anywhere without a prescription.
- It's free.

CAN YOUR WORDS MAKE OTHERS LAUGH?

So we now know two important things about laughter. The first one we've known since early childhood—it always feels good to laugh. Second, there's a mountain of scientific evidence suggesting that it's good for our health. This is proof that we should be making each other laugh as much as possible. Are we all capable of doing this? The answer is yes!

I'm not claiming that we all have equal talent for saying funny things. We can't all be Robin Williams, Eddie Murphy, Woody Allen, Bill Cosby, or Jerry Seinfeld, but we *can* be agents of laughter by doing a few simple things:

Be on the lookout for humor. It often comes from unexpected places. There's a world of comedy all around us. I suggested earlier that we become "good finders" so we'll have something positive to talk about. I would also suggest that we become "funny finders." Humor is all around us and is always worth sharing. But we have to find it first.

Write it down in a designated place. I maintain two humor folders. One I keep in my briefcase. When I'm traveling and see, read, or hear something funny, I write it down and put it in the folder. The other folder I keep next to my computer. When friends send me funny stuff over the Internet, I print it out (some of it) and save it in that folder. It's amazing how large these two folders have gotten and what a huge storehouse of good clean humor I now have.

Subscribe to sources of humor. There are a number of print publications that are either devoted entirely to humor or have a humor section. There are also a variety of Internet websites and services that provide comic relief. I subscribe to Joke of the Day and look forward to opening my e-mail each morning because I know I'll get at least two clean jokes and a one-liner. There are also humor columns in many newspapers. Over the years I've saved many hilarious pieces written by people like Dave Barry, Andy Rooney, Maureen Dowd, Molly Ivins, Argus Hamilton, and others. There are also several books available that contain many of the favorite jokes, stories, and one-liners of some of the funniest people in the country.

Share what's funny with others. I often hear people say, "I can't tell a joke." Some jokes require a certain style and delivery, and we can't all tell them like the professional comedians do, but we can all share funny things. Many years ago I heard a comedy writer talk about the importance of humor and laughter in every-day life. He said each of us should always have at least five funny things to share with others. He suggested finding five jokes, puns, stories, quotes, etc., that we're comfortable with, writing down key words about them on a small card to trigger the memory, and carrying it with us in a purse or wallet. As we find something new and better, add it to the card, replacing one of the others. It's amazing how this simple technique can both keep us on the look-out for good humor and keep us well stocked with it.

A COLLECTION OF FUNNIES

Since I've been collecting humor for years, this chapter seems to be the perfect place to share some of it. Keep in mind that not all people think the same things are funny, but most of these have passed the test with speaking audiences. Also, humor on paper is often quite different from humor that's spoken, but most of these work both ways. I should add that my favorite type of humor is what I call "unexpected and unintended"—people saying or writing things in a serious vein, but they come out funny. Most of my examples are of this type and are divided into categories. I've either come across them myself or they were sent to me by readers. By all means, share them with others.

Want Ads

Doberman pincher: smart, young, strong, good guard dog, eats anything, loves children.

For sale: antique desk suitable for lady with thick legs and big drawers.

Now is your chance to have your ears pierced and get an extra pair to take home, too.

Seeking employment: Tired of cleaning yourself? Let me do it instead.

Seeking employment: Man, honest. Will take anything.

Used cars: Why go elsewhere and be cheated? Come here first.

Child care: Our experienced Mom will care for your child. Fenced yard, meals, and smacks included.

Illiterate? Write today for free help.

Signs

In a Georgia public park:

All dogs and some children should be kept on a leash.

On a New York convalescent home:

For the sick and tired of the Episcopal church

On a Maine shop:

Our goal is to give our customers the lowest possible prices and workmanship.

On a highway sign in Arizona:

State Prison Ahead. Do not stop for hitchhikers.

On a highway sign in Texas:

Hitchhikers may be escaped convicts. [The sign was riddled with bulletholes.]

In the office of a loan company:

Ask about our plans for owning your home.

In a New York coffee shop:

Customers who consider our waitresses rude should see the manager.

Near a diner/gas station in Indiana:

Eat here and get gas.

In the window of a Kentucky appliance store:

Don't kill your wife. Let our washing machine do the dirty work.

In the window of an Oklahoma photo shop:

Have the kids shot for Dad from $24.95.

On a Chicago radiator repair shop:

Best place to take a leak.

Seen everywhere:

Slow children at play.

Church Bulletins

Little Mothers meeting this Wed. night. All ladies interested in becoming Little Mothers should see the pastor in his study.

Irving Benson and Jessie Carter were married on October 24 in the church. So ends a friendship that began in their school days.

Eight new choir robes are currently needed due to addition of several new members and to the deterioration of some older ones.

Miss Charlene Mason sang, "I will not pass this way again," giving obvious pleasure to the congregation.

Barbara remains in the hospital and needs blood donors for more transfusions. She is also having trouble sleeping and requests tapes of Pastor Jack's sermons.

The rector will preach his farewell message after which the choir will sing "Break Forth into Joy."

Ladies, don't forget the rummage sale. It's a chance to get rid of those things not worth keeping around the house. Don't forget to bring your husbands.

A bean supper will be held on Tuesday evening in the church hall. Music will follow.

At the evening service tonight, the sermon topic will be "What is Hell?" Come early and listen to the choir practice.

Smile at someone who is hard to love.

Sign outside a church:

Don't let worry kill you. Let the church help.

Newspaper Headlines

Milk drinkers are turning to powder

New study of obesity looks for larger test group

Dr. Ruth to talk about sex with newspaper reporters

Grandmother of eight makes hole in one

Police begin campaign to run down jaywalkers

Safety experts say school bus passengers should be belted

Farmer Bill Dies in House

Queen Mary to have bottom scraped

Dealers will hear car talk at noon

Bumper Stickers

Honk if you love peace and quiet

The early bird gets the worm, but the second mouse gets the cheese

Everyone has a photographic memory; some don't have any film

My son was Inmate of the Month at San Mateo County Jail

Hard work has a future. Laziness pays off now!

They're not hot flashes; they're power surges!

Where there's a will . . . I want to be in it

Children's humor

Little kids think almost everything is funny. That's why they laugh a lot more than adults do. But they're often at their funniest when they're just being their innocent selves. Here are some examples.

Actual letters to pastors

Dear Pastor: . . .

. . . I know God loves everybody, but He never met my sister.

. . . I would like to go to heaven some day because I know my brother won't be there.

. . . Please pray for all the airline pilots. I am flying to California tomorrow.

. . . Please say a prayer for our Little League team. We need God's help or a new pitcher.

. . . My father says I should learn the 10 Commandments. But I don't think I want to because we have enough rules already in the house.

. . . Are there any devils on earth? I think there may be one in my class.

. . . I liked your sermon on Sunday. Especially when it was done.

Sentence completion by children

Don't bite the hand that . . . looks dirty.

Strike while the . . . bug is close.

An idle mind is . . . the best way to relax.

A penny saved is . . . not much.

You can't teach an old dog new . . . math.

Better be safe than . . . punch a fifth grader.

It's always darkest right before . . . daylight savings time.

Children should be seen and not . . . spanked or grounded.

Laugh and the world laughs with you, cry and . . . you have to blow your nose.

—CONTRIBUTED BY DEB BROWN, AN AWARD-WINNING
ELEMENTARY SCHOOL TEACHER IN WEST VIRGINIA

Some personal favorites

In the late 1990s, I conducted an all-day workshop at a summer Character Education conference in New York. Robin Genet, a third-grade teacher from New Hampshire, stayed afterward to thank me for sharing what she considered to be some practical strategies for the classroom. She said she was eager for school to start so she could try them. I gave her my address and asked her to send me some feedback about a month into the school year. The following October I received a letter from Robin and a packet of letters from her third-grade students. All of them were wonderful, but one stood out. The letter on top of the packet opened this way: "I don't know what you did with Miss Genet in New York, but she sure came back to school in a good mood."

Tracy Gotch, a fourth-grade teacher in the Sacramento area, helps her students read my book *Life's Greatest Lessons* each year. They read a little at a time, do activities related to each chapter, and hold class discussions. This process starts in September and ends in April. Tracy then has the children write letters to me about how they benefited from the book. The first year she did this, a little girl in the class wrote the following: "I think I've become a better person since we read your book, and my mother thinks so, too. She is very nice and pretty and single. Are you married?"

I lived three miles north of the high school I taught at, so I had a short commute. One of the buildings I drove past each morning was the Church of the Nazarene, a small church set back from the road but with a large marquee out in front. The pastor changed his message each week, and because it was always something clever (usually rhyming), I paid close attention on Monday morning to see what his new message was. One day it read, "If you're tired of sin, come on in." I got a chuckle out of it. It wasn't hilarious, but it was cute, and consistent with his pattern. I drove past it for three days, then noticed on Thursday that some words had been added to the sign by someone equally clever. The sign now read: "If you're tired of sin, come on in. If you're not, call 555-9874."

One of my colleagues received the following note from a parent excusing her daughter from school the previous day due to illness: "Maryann was absent on Tuesday because she had a fever and upset stomach. Her sister was also sick, and her brother had a fever. I wasn't too well either. There must be something going around. Her father even got hot last night."

Early in my teaching career, I was giving a test in my U.S. history class on the Civil War. We had spent a long time on Abraham Lincoln and the Emancipation Proclamation. I always put the easiest questions at the beginning of the test, so the easiest of all was the first one: "What was the famous document signed by Abraham Lincoln during the Civil War that was intended to end slavery?" One of my students, not trying to be funny and simply getting a word mixed up, answered, "The Emancipation Constipation."

I had my high school seniors write one hundred lifetime goals at the completion of a lengthy unit I taught them on goal setting. Near the end of my career, I read the goals of a seventeen-year-old girl who had planned a lot of adventure for her years after high school. She was going to travel the world and do a lot of exciting things. Goal 100? "Retire and play bingo."

Victor Borge once said, "Laughter is the shortest distance between two people." There's great wisdom in that simple statement. There are so many things we can say to friends, colleagues, family members, even strangers to make them feel good. One of the best ways is to make them laugh. While we can't all be great comedians, we can look for, find, and share funny things. Laughter is a critical part of the human survival kit.

Among those whom I like or admire I can find no common denominator, but among those whom I love, I can: all of them make me laugh.

—W. H. AUDEN

Humor is a serious thing. I like to think of it as one of our greatest natural resources which must be preserved at all costs.

—JAMES THURBER

Part Three

Four Places Where Positive Words Can Work Wonders

No matter where we are—the factory, the playground, the office, the school, the church, the dinner party, the boardroom, the gym, the poker game—words will be spoken, and they will affect us.

—Erwin G. Hall

CHAPTER 11

———

AFFECTIONATE WORDS
BUILD STRONG FAMILIES

Strong families emphasize that good communication doesn't necessarily happen; it usually takes time and practice.

—NICK STINNETT AND JOHN DEFRAIN

TEN WAYS THAT WORDS CAN ENRICH FAMILY LIFE

There's no place in the world where words are more important than in the family. It's the bedrock of any society, and it's where our children first learn how to communicate and interact with others. It's also where they learn *what* to say and *how* to say it. They learn these things from their first teachers—their parents and the other adults with whom they have the most contact in their formative years.

For many years I've been making presentations throughout the United States and in other countries to families associated with various schools and places of worship. The title of the presentation is almost always the same: "Raising Good Kids: 10 suggestions for parents." And the focus is always on language used in the family. The most important suggestion I make to parents is this: *Spend quality time together.* Reduced to a nutshell, that's what most determines whether a family will be healthy or dysfunctional. And what most determines the quality of that time together is the language used—what people in the family say to one another and how they say it. So my ten suggestions here all have to do with using words to build a strong and loving family, particularly those with children.

1. Model the language you want your children to use

In Chapter 8, I made some suggestions regarding communication among couples. They're equally valid for couples with children. However, if there are kids in the home, no matter what their ages, then the way the adults talk to each other takes on added significance. One thing parents always need to be aware of is that they're teaching their children something every time they open their mouths.

Children, especially little ones, are great imitators. They do what they see done by the dominant adults in their lives, and they repeat what they hear those adults say. Whether they live with a single parent, the traditional mom and dad, an extended family, or one of the many other possible combinations, they're listening and learning to form their speech patterns. If the adults in their lives are talking to them, to another adult, or on the phone, or commenting on world affairs, they're picking up signals and learning how to talk.

If these adults frequently swear, put each other down, complain, gossip, criticize, and yell, there's a high probability that the kids will do the same. The more these are done, the more they're reinforced. An example drawn from my own childhood:

Although it was many years ago and I was only in the first grade, I remember it vividly. My father, who had a short temper and a loud voice, had become angry with a customer in our store. He literally chased the man out of the building and, in the process, not only told him to never come back but also to "go to hell."

I thought that was the coolest thing I'd ever heard and couldn't wait to try it out on one of my friends. So the next morning on the playground at school, my best buddy asked me if I wanted to play kickball. He was more than a little surprised when my answer was, "Go to hell." I felt so proud—and so adult. And I was sure that I had impressed all the kids within earshot. But before I found out just how impressed they were, I learned that my teacher, a very strict nun, was not impressed at all. In fact, she was shocked. She asked, "*What* did you say?" And before I could answer I was given a solid thumping. (Keep in mind that this was back in the days of corporal punishment.) It dawned on me, even at the tender age of six, that maybe it wasn't all that cool to tell people to "go to hell," even if you did hear your dad say it. Actually, my story is pretty mild compared to what young children are hearing today. I often shudder at some of the things I hear parents say to their kids while out in public.

But there's a flip side—a positive one—to this also. Many parents and guardians are not only aware of the impact of language on formative minds, they're making a conscious effort to model and teach the use of kind and nurturing words. Good parents are careful with their words and the tone in which they speak, not only to each other but also to their children. They use clean and gentle language and generally focus their conversations on what's good in the world.

Maybe these adults are reading some of the many outstanding parenting books that are currently available. I've looked at more than twenty in the past year and found several common threads that run through all of them. One is kind and affirming language.

It sets the tone and creates an atmosphere in the home in which children flourish. No matter what's going on outside the home and no matter what the entertainment media is broadcasting, the consistently gentle words of a parent are far more powerful. These types of parents are the best teachers of all.

Children Learn What They Live
If children live with criticism, they learn to condemn.
If children live with shame, they learn to feel guilty.

If children live with encouragement, they learn confidence.
If children live with praise, they learn appreciation.
—DOROTHY LAW NOLTE

2. Read to your children

One of the best ways that parents can strengthen family ties and simultaneously teach sound moral principles is to read to—and with—their children.
—HELEN R. LeGETTE

No one knows for sure who the first parent was to read bedtime stories to his or her children. It was probably a frustrated mother who couldn't get her child to calm down, so she pulled out a book and soothed the child with a good story. We do know that this practice began hundreds of years ago and that it had a powerful effect on both the child and the parent. It was done long before there was such a thing as a child psychologist, yet it's one of the top recommendations they've been making to parents for years. The earlier, the better, they advise.

Several years ago there was a survey taken among people who

were well-known for both their achievements and for their community spirit. One of the questions was, "What childhood experiences had the greatest influence on your life?" There were many different answers pertaining to nurturing parental practices, but the most common response by far was, "My parents read to me at night."

The benefits of this simple practice of reading to a child, if done regularly, are immeasurable. And now that it's been so thoroughly studied, the most important results are well established and documented.

It bonds the child and the parent both physically and emotionally.

The parent is usually on the bed, and the physical contact gives the child feelings of warmth and security. The shared stories usually lead to questions and comments by the child, which lead to meaningful conversation and emotional closeness.

It introduces the child to great literature and powerful stories with a moral message.

Traditionally, parents who read to their children select classic stories that are well written and contain a message that focuses on positive character traits. This gives the child a great appreciation for both, and it increases the probability that he or she will be influenced by them in the latter stages of life. There is no shortage of great bedtime reading materials for parents to choose from. They range from Bill Bennett's *The Book of Virtues* to Jim Trelease's *The Read-Aloud Handbook* to Louise Knapp's *The Little Engine That Could*. Libraries and bookstores have these and hundreds of other valuable collections of stories.

It fosters a love of reading in the child.

Research shows that children who are read to are far more likely to read for both pleasure and information as adults. This is also a great antidote to some of the not-so-healthy materials the media bombards children with. These children not only become better readers but also develop their imaginations. They also become better-informed citizens.

It leads to success in school.
The National Commission on Reading, after researching the topic extensively, concluded that "the single most important contribution parents can make toward their children's success in school is to read aloud to them." At a time when our nation is demanding educational accountability and high test scores, parents have a way to offer invaluable assistance.

There are several other benefits of reading to children. Among them are learning, inexpensive entertainment, meaningful conversation, moral lessons, and improved writing skills. No matter how we look at it, it always results in win-win.

> *You may have tangible wealth untold; Caskets of jewels and coffers of gold. Richer than I you can never be—I had a mother who read to me.*
> —Strickland Gillian

Note to fathers: it's perfectly okay for you to read to your children. In fact, you should be doing at least half of it.

3. Have meaningful conversation

A few years ago, an organization called TV-Free America, along with help from the A. C. Nielsen Company, famous for its television ratings, conducted an extensive survey on American families. While the main focus of the study had to do with television-viewing habits, there were other significant findings. Here are two rather amazing statistics from this study:

- Number of minutes per week that the average child watches television: 1,680 (28 hours)
- Number of minutes per week that parents spend in meaningful conversation with their children: 3.5

One of the main problems in American families in recent years has been lack of time together. A variety of social and economic changes in our society have brought this about. The result is that families are spending less and less time together and, therefore, less and less time talking to each other. Nothing binds people together more than heart-to-heart conversation. But, unfortunately, this isn't taking place in a frighteningly high percentage of families.

Parents need to make face-to-face meaningful conversation a high priority. If it isn't, the family routine too often becomes similar to ships passing in the night. Many families are now so scattered that members spend more time talking to each other on their cell phones than they do talking in person. During my last five years of high school teaching, a majority of my students reported that they rarely saw their parents during the week. When I asked them why, I received answers such as, "We're all on the go," "We're scattered," "We're just too busy."

The old saying is that, "We can always find time for the things that are important to us." Like most old sayings, it's true. Nothing is more important in a family than meaningful conversation—between adult and adult, between adult and child, and between child and child. Strong, cohesive families have consistently good dialogue on an ongoing basis. They establish it as a priority, and they build it into their routine. A few simple suggestions will be made later in this chapter.

4. Ask good questions

Here's the most common question parents ask their children: "What did you learn in school today?" It's asked literally millions of times each day. Remarkably, about 99.9 percent of the time this famous question receives exactly the same answer: "Nuthin'" End of conversation. Ask a bad question, get a bad answer. School and learning are topics that should be discussed in every family every evening, but for the conversation to become meaningful, it needs to begin with better questions.

In my presentations to parents and to teachers, I always try to remind them that they're partners in raising and teaching children. The more they communicate, especially about what's going on in school, the better the questions will be at home. Parents have a responsibility to know both the subjects being taught and the other programs going on at the school. This kind of knowledge leads to good questions, better answers, and much improved conversation. It can also be fun and informative. It's amazing how many interesting things (in addition to how to operate a computer) small children can teach their parents and how good they feel when they do it.

5. Celebrate the day at the dinner table

Obviously, a family can't have good conversation at the dinner table unless it's *at* the dinner table. Unfortunately, this is another American family tradition that has seriously deteriorated. In a study done in 2000, it was reported that less than forty percent of American families regularly eat dinner together. Of the families that do eat dinner together, two-thirds of them do so with the television on. If they're not at the table together, or are at the table with the TV on, there isn't going to be a lot of good conversation.

Because I grew up in an era in which virtually all families ate dinner together, I maintained the same tradition in my family. I was a single father with three sons for ten years. One of the things I noticed as the kids got older was that they wanted to spend less time at the dinner table. They wanted to bolt their food down and get out and play. But I insisted that it be a time of family sharing. Since the kids weren't all that keen on the idea, I felt it was my responsibility to come up with topics that would hold their interest.

I came up with an absolutely brilliant idea: the Question of the Night. I would ask my sons who their favorite teacher was, what their favorite subject was, what their favorite sport was, etc. The Question of the Night remained brilliant for about two weeks. It was then that the question supply began to approach the empty mark. It became harder and harder to come up with something good every night, and I realized that we had a lot of years together ahead. It became more difficult than preparing a new lesson plan daily for each subject I taught.

One night while I was preparing dinner (probably one of my hot dog specials), I kept drawing blanks on a good question. The kids had grown to like it, so as soon as we all sat down, one of them asked, "So, Dad, what's the Question of the Night?" I had to admit to them that my system had developed a flaw (better known as lack of imagination) and that I didn't have one. I'm not sure how this popped into my head, but I said, "Instead of a question, how about if you each tell me what was the best thing that happened to you to-day? What was the highlight of your day?" Purely by accident—and out of desperation—I had stumbled on the Magic Question!

The kids all had something funny, heartwarming, or interesting to share. They also wanted to know what my highlight was. Over the years they learned a lot about my teaching career and about why I enjoyed it so much, and I learned about the things that were important to them. The best part was that the Magic Question could be asked every night. I didn't have to wrack my brain coming up with a new one, and I was guaranteed to get positive answers. We celebrated the day every night at the dinner table.

6. Catch your kids doing something right

Believe it or not, kids do more things right than they do wrong. But which do they hear about more frequently? Most of them hear about every one of their screw-ups but very little about their good deeds. It's one of the most common mistakes parents make, and it's been going on for generations. The sad truth is that most parents are better at catching their kids doing something wrong than they are at catching them doing something right.

I was one of these parents until getting stopped in my tracks one day by my oldest son, Dan. I had just come home and pointed out to him that he had left his dishes on the kitchen counter that morning before leaving for school. Dan had either been having a bad day or he just couldn't take any more of my faultfinding. His eyes welled up with tears and he blurted out, "All you ever do is tell me what I do wrong." His words penetrated. They indicted me, and I was guilty as charged. Tears filled my own eyes because I shamefully realized at that moment that I had been doing with my children what my own father had done with me. I had become an expert in catching them doing things wrong.

As I looked at the tears in my son's eyes and heard the frustration in his voice, I wanted to undo all the criticism and replace it with praise, but I couldn't. It dawned on me that I had a great kid. He was polite, was a good student, helped around the house, was a good athlete, was a hard worker, and stayed out of trouble. Any parent would be happy and proud to have a son like this. And what was he telling his dad? "All you ever do is tell me what I do wrong."

Our family life changed dramatically on that day. I had a long talk with Dan and his brothers. I admitted my errors, asked for their forgiveness, and promised to do everything within my power to let them know how much I appreciated them and how proud I was of them. It made a remarkable difference, mainly because my children finally heard some things that all children need to hear from their parents from time to time. It's healthy for us to admit that we're wrong and to say we're sorry. It's even healthier to acknowledge and thank our kids when they do the right thing.

As painful as it is, I tell this story every time I speak to groups of parents. I tell it because it resonates with so many of them. Even some of the most loving and caring parents fall into the trap of focusing too much on the wrongdoings of their children. I also tell the story because we learn from our mistakes. It helps other parents realize that they're doing the same thing I did and that they can correct it and improve their family life at any time. Our kids, like everyone else, love to be acknowledged for the good things they do.

7. Correct gently

While we need to do a better job of catching our kids doing the right thing, we also have the responsibility of correcting them when they violate family rules or do something that's not in their best interest. The key is *how* we do it. Family therapists tell us that jarring criticism of children is one of the most common mistakes parents make. If it's done harshly and with destructive words, it can do far more harm than whatever the child did wrong. But if done gently and with reassuring words, it can help the child grow. Family therapists also tell us that constructive and gentle criticism (along with catching our kids doing right) is one of the most important responsibilities of a parent.

In a nutshell, here are the worst things a parent can do when a child does something wrong:

- Explode verbally without thinking first.
- Yell and scream.
- Threaten.
- Call the child names.
- Focus on the person rather than on the act.

Our kids *will* do things wrong. It always has been, and always will be, a great challenge for parents to deal with it in an effective manner. The responses listed above make the situation worse. The ones below help both the child and the parent resolve the issue:

- Literally count to ten to give yourself time to think about what you're going to say and how you're going to say it.
- Keep your voice at a normal volume.
- Reassure the child. Example: "Jennifer, we love you very much, but what you did is wrong and we need to talk about it."
- Focus on the wrongdoing, not the person who did it.
- Forgive the child.

8. Use and teach the magic words

Just as children do not inherit good character, they do not inherit good manners. They must be taught.
—HELEN R. LeGETTE

Manners will become important to children only if they are important to their parents.
—THOMAS LICKONA

For hundreds of years the magic words "please" and "thank you," along with a number of other terms of courtesy, were taught and modeled in virtually every home. They were reinforced in schools and in places of worship, and the result was a polite and civil society. This began to change in the mid 1960s for a variety of reasons. While good manners are still stressed by many parents, it

can no longer be assumed that most children are learning them in
the home.

Nowhere is this more evident than in our schools. Many educators are now trying to teach children the manners they should
be learning in the home. As an educator for many years, I can
relate to their predicament. Many of my teenage students told me
that they didn't say "please" in school or in other places because
they got what they wanted at home *without* saying it. They also
informed me that they didn't say "thank you" because it was
unnecessary. They already had what they wanted.

Fortunately, I also had a lot of gracious and polite kids who
had been taught the magic words at home. When asked about
their parents' method of teaching good manners, virtually all of
the kids said things similar to these:

- "My parents always spoke politely to one another and to
  us, and they did the same outside the home."
- "They kept reminding us to say 'please' and 'thank you'
  until it became a habit."
- "They taught us that people who use polite language
  become more successful and have more friends."
- "My parents told us they were proud of us when we
  were polite to other people without being told."

All are sound advice.

9. Write a family mission statement about words in the home

All great organizations have a mission statement—a brief declaration
of purpose that helps keep its members focused and reminds them
of their responsibilities. How about a family mission statement for
the same reason? Since communication in a family is the lifeblood of
it, how about a mission statement that focuses on language?

A few years ago I read an article by a man whose two children were going through that nasty "put-down" stage. They argued and ripped on each other constantly, and it was making life at home very unpleasant. Mom and Dad called for a family meeting to discuss the problem. Their main point was that the world can be a harsh place in which we too often get criticized or put down. We should all have a sanctuary—a safe place in which we can feel protected from the verbal arrows that pierce us on the outside. That sanctuary should be the home.

Instead of threatening the kids with punishment, the parents asked them to help find a solution. After an hour of productive brainstorming, they came up with the idea of a family mission statement addressing the issue. It read: "Home is where we build one another." They printed it out in large script letters on their computer, had it framed, and hung it in their kitchen. They also made a commitment to live by their statement. The results were astounding. This is what a family problem-solving session, a mission statement, and a commitment can do.

I've shared that story with every parent organization I've spoken to for the last ten years. Each time I challenge them to do the same. The feedback has been tremendously heartwarming. Some of the families have used the one I shared with them. Others have written their own. Here are a couple of my favorites:

- No put-downs—compliments spoken here.
- Who has something good to say?
- This family celebrates—life and one another.

10. Schedule a family night

"The best decision I ever made regarding the usage of my time was to schedule a weekly one-hour family night. The positive and lasting impact this has had on each of us is immeasurable." This statement was made by a time efficiency expert at a retreat I attended a few years ago. Most of the people at the retreat were executives in the business world, and they were looking for ways to get more work done in less time. But they went away with something far more valuable: a plan to spend more quality time with their families.

There were only four rules regarding family night:

1. It would be at the same time and same day each week.
2. It would be held even if a family member was absent.
3. It would be a minimum of one hour in length.
4. The activity had to include conversation.

The workshop leader, who is not a Mormon, said he got the idea from one of his Mormon friends because it's a regular practice in that faith. He said initially there was resistance by his kids, then six, eight, and twelve. But within a few months, it became evident that family night was something special. Each family member took turns deciding what the activity would be, so the other members came to the meeting not knowing what to expect. That was part of the fun. He said his kids often surprised him. Sometimes they would teach the rest of the family something they had learned at school, sometimes they would play a game, sometimes they would ask a thought-provoking question, sometimes they would share a meaningful quote. There was a wide variety of activities, each one resulting in a special bonding that increased weekly.

"You gotta do this!" he said excitedly. "Next to worshipping together, it's the best thing our family does. We had a good family before we started doing this. Now we have a great family." Talk to any parent or any kid whose family does this and you'll hear the same thing. One hour a week can make a huge difference and create memories that will last forever.

Healthy families require healthy communication.
—H. NORMAN WRIGHT

Every word that parents and their children speak, every action that parents and their children take, and every deed that parents and their children perform help to create the children's "memory bank." That record—that memory bank—becomes the parents' history and posterity. For the children, it is their inheritance and their destiny.

—Rabbi Wayne Dosick

CHAPTER 12

GENTLE WORDS
TEACH KINDNESS
IN OUR SCHOOLS

As one afflicted with feelings of inferiority and poor self-esteem as a youth, I am particularly sensitive to the importance of caring, love, encouragement and praise from those whose lives touch mine. Encouragement and praise . . . have the power to change a life, and that life may in turn change others.

—NORMAN VINCENT PEALE

NO PUT-DOWNS
COMPLIMENTS SPOKEN HERE

The words above are from a large sign that was prominently displayed in the front of my classroom for many years. It was one of the first things anyone entering the room noticed. The "No Put-downs" part of the sign was inside the familiar red circle with the slash through it. The "Compliments Spoken Here" part was in large letters underneath the circle. It was one of many signs in the front of the room, but it was the only one I made special mention of on the first day of school. I did it because I wanted to be proactive and to set the tone early. Just as a home should be a sanctuary, so should a classroom. It needs to be a place where students feel safe, welcome, and part of a caring community. In fact, this is the way students should feel about the entire school. But, unfortunately, this is not always the case.

"WHEN SCHOOL HURTS"

This was a headline in *USA Today* on April 10, 2001. The article, a thoroughly researched and well-written piece by Karen Peterson, reminds us that school can too often be a scary, painful, and lonely place for many students in virtually any grade. The number one cause of these feelings of alienation is harmful words. They come from other students in many forms: intimidation, threats, name-calling, teasing, put-downs, and racial and sexual slurs. These kinds of comments hurt more than being hit or kicked, and the wounds take much longer to heal.

Consider the following statistics:

- More than 160,000 children stay home from school each day because of verbal intimidation and put-downs by their peers.
- More than two-thirds of all our students are teased or gossiped about at school at least once a month.
- Almost one-third of students between grades six and ten (5.7 million children nationwide) have been bullied at school.
- Virtually all of the thirty-seven serious violent attacks in our schools between the years 1976 and 2001 were the direct result of verbal put-downs and intimidation.

There are a number of theories on why this is happening, but there are two far more important issues that school leaders need to be concerned with: (1) What can we learn from the findings of this research? and (2) Can we teach children to use language more constructively, and, in turn, improve the climate in our schools?

Lessons from Columbine and other school shootings

The most painful lesson, yet possibly the most valuable, came from the tragic shooting deaths at Columbine High School in the Denver area in the spring of 1999. Because it was the worst-ever act of violence in a school, it got more media attention and follow-up investigation than any previous incident. We learned that in the culture of a large public high school in an upper-middle-class neighborhood, there was little or no tolerance for those who were "different." If you were out of the mainstream of the student society, you were reminded about it every day in the form of taunts by your peers. This had a cumulative effect, and each day's verbal abuse was piled onto that of the day before . . . and the countless days before that. The result was a disaster and a national nightmare.

In the aftermath of the tragedy, we learned that the insults had been going on for a long time. Educators at the school were aware of it, but little was done to put an end to it. "Kids will be kids" was the prevailing philosophy, and the abuse continued until the shootings. I'm not suggesting that all verbal abuse in school will lead to murder, but we do know that virtually all of the other school shootings had the same cause. Whether kids bring a gun to school or not, they're being hurt in horrific ways by the unthinking and often mean-spirited comments of their peers.

Eric Harris, one of the students involved in the Columbine shootings, left a suicide note. It was an e-mail addressed to the parents of the many students he intended to kill. He wrote to them: "Your children, who have ridiculed me, who have chosen not to accept me, who have treated me like I am not worth their time, are dead." A classmate had this to say about Dylan Klebold, the other student involved in the shootings: "He really felt unloved. He wasn't so bad. He was lonely." These were kids who were hurt by their peers, by words that had become deadly weapons. So they responded with their own weapons.

The principal at Columbine, interviewed by the news media as the school was reopening four months later, acknowledged that school officials had not been sensitive enough to the kind of social ostracism felt by Harris, Klebold, and other students who were outside the mainstream of the school culture. He also announced that the school would have a new "zero tolerance" policy toward all forms of verbal harassment.

If there's one thing school leaders should learn from this tragic event, it's to tune in to what students are saying to one another and to the effect that it's having. We can no longer excuse it by claiming that this is something all kids do and that they've been doing it for as long as kids have existed. Even if this is true, we're called upon to do everything we can to stop kids from hurting each other in our schools, just as parents have the same responsibility at home.

The Columbine principal's "zero tolerance" policy regarding put-downs, teasing, etc., sounded good, especially under the circumstances, but it won't work. While well-intentioned, it's reactive, shortsighted, and impossible to enforce. Instead of waiting for something tragic to happen, school leaders need to take proactive steps at the beginning of each school year (and reinforce them regularly) regarding the power of words. All adults who work at the school, all the students, and all the parents should be involved. It may sound like an insurmountable task in a large public school, but it isn't. The good news is that we've learned much from the research, and there are now schools all over the country that are serving as excellent models of safe, caring, and nurturing environments.

When Words Are Win-Win

There are programs that promote positive language now operating successfully all over the country. Many are schoolwide plans that have dramatically improved campus climate, while others are the ingenious ideas of dedicated and caring classroom teachers. There are four main results:

1. Kids of all ages become more aware of the power of their words either to tear down or build up.
2. The use of hurtful language is dramatically reduced.
3. The use of kind and affirming words is dramatically increased.
4. The school becomes a caring community in which kids feel safe and are being nurtured by both their teachers and their peers.

Here are a few samples of teaching kids to make healthy choices with their words.

No Put-downs

This is a national program available to schools everywhere. It defines "put-downs" as "negative or belittling words or actions that show disrespect toward a person or groups of persons." Some of the key principles of this highly effective program:

- All members of the school or individual classrooms are responsible for creating a respectful environment.
- Youth are a resource, not a problem. They can make important contributions to the school community. In fact, they *are* the community.
- Violence can be prevented when members of the community learn the necessary skills together. These skills

include clear communication, self-control, supportive behavior, and constructive response to conflict.

Positive word power

This is a simple activity that can be used with kids of almost any age. It's described by Dr. Thomas Lickona in his powerful book, *Educating for Character: How Our Schools Can Teach Respect and Responsibility.* He asks students to help him make a list of words we can say to other people that are likely to give them good feelings. After that's complete, he asks them to do the opposite: write down words that are likely to give other people bad feelings. Students are able to come up with several words in both categories within minutes. He then asks them, "So words have power, don't they?" They agree. He then reminds them that every time they speak to others, they have the power to make someone feel good or bad. He also asks them which words they would rather hear about themselves and which ones they don't like to hear.

This is followed up with an activity in which the students write positive words on slips of paper about their classmates. These slips are eventually distributed to each student, and a meaningful conversation follows. All kids benefit from the exercise and become more aware of two important aspects of communication with their peers: (1) words are choices, and (2) positive words almost always create a win-win situation. Kids also realize that it feels good to be the senders of positive words. Dr. Lickona explains this simple yet powerful activity as he did it with fifth graders. I used a variation of it for many years with eleventh and twelfth graders. The value of it is immeasurable.

"In this school, we don't talk like that"

Dr. David Brooks has held a wide variety of positions within schools, including principal. He's also a pioneer in Character

Education and one of the top presenters in the field. He was at a middle school several years ago that had a serious problem with students using filthy language. It was heard all over the campus, and reprimands and punishments seemed to have no effect. Faculty members wanted to correct the problem but were stymied, and many had given up. After meeting with Dr. Brooks and a consultant, the teachers agreed to try a new approach. Each time a staff member heard a student use profanity, he or she would approach the student, say "In this school, we don't talk like that," and then walk away.

The most important aspect of this strategy was that all staff members did it consistently. They sent a direct message to the kids, and they reinforced one another in their effort to clean up the language at the school. It worked. Within a few weeks, the use of profanity on campus had been almost eliminated. What pleased the staff members the most was that the kids began to police themselves regarding inappropriate language. Within a short time, students were saying the same thing to newcomers who used foul words: "In this school, we don't talk like that."

The key in this case was establishing expectations. Something many of us learned in Sociology 1A was that people behave as they're expected to behave. In this case, expectations were made clear in a brief and nonconfrontational manner, and the school climate improved dramatically.

An Emily Dickinson classic makes a point with kids

Alice Hazel is one of those teachers we'd all want our children to have. She's taught English in a middle school in the Buffalo area for many years and still loves her job and the kids. She's designed a great lesson about the power of words around a well-known poem by Emily Dickinson.

*   *   *

A Word

A word is dead
When it is said,
Some say.

I say it just
Begins to live
That day.

Alice begins by having her students read the poem and then discusses it with them. Then they write about two incidents on separate sheets of paper. On one, they describe an incident that they witnessed, caused, or experienced in which someone said something hurtful to another person. On the other sheet, they write about an incident in which a compliment or a kind word was spoken. The students put their sheets in two separate boxes without signing their names.

Alice asks all the students to take one sheet from each box. She then divides the class into small groups so they can discuss each situation. Since these are real incidents about the positive and negative impact of words, and because they come from classmates, the kids take the assignment seriously. They share their insights with one another, and they all have an opportunity to express their feelings. Feedback from both her students and their parents lets her know that this simple exercise has a positive and lasting effect.

Replacement words

Madeline Turner is another teacher who knows how to connect with kids and understands the importance of teaching them how to connect without using offensive words. She teaches at-risk kids in a public high school in Marietta, Georgia. Many of her students have developed some bad verbal habits (swearing, put-downs, complaining) long before they enter her class. School policy requires her to write up students who use inappropriate language and send them to the dean.

She thought there should be a better way of dealing with this problem, one that was more likely to lead to a solution than it was to punishment, required a little creativity, and didn't waste a lot of time. So she made a deal with her students: She wouldn't write them up or send them anywhere if they would immediately restate any offensive word that slipped out with a "replacement word." Example: One of her students gets upset about something and, without thinking, yells out the famous "f" word. Madeline will look at him and calmly say, "I need a replacement word." A quick replacement word will keep the kid out of more serious trouble, so he immediately comes up with something like "fudge." It usually gets a laugh—from the offending student himself, from the other students within earshot, and from Madeline. Results: The problem was dealt with immediately, the student had an opportunity to correct his offensive language, a lesson was learned, and they all got back to business.

These are only a few of the many effective strategies being used in schools to help kids think before they talk and to choose words that help create a safe and positive learning environment. They show us that it can be done. Notice that the students weren't just *told* to use kind words. They were given an opportunity to be on both the sending and receiving ends of this type of communication. They grasp the win-win concept quickly when they have this opportunity.

THE IMPACT OF TEACHERS

Teachers, by the very nature of their jobs, talk more than anyone. Because of that and because they're given the responsibility of molding young minds, they should be as careful with their words as parents should be. For the most part, they're outstanding in this regard. There are exceptions, of course, and even the best and most affirming teachers admit that they need to be reminded often of the magnitude of their words.

Near the beginning of every presentation I make to teachers and other people who work in our schools, I share a powerful quote with them. It's one I kept taped to my desk at school under a plastic coating so it would be the first thing I saw each morning. It served as a daily reminder of the awesome responsibility of a teacher.

The Difference a Teacher Can Make

I have come to the frightening conclusion that I am the decisive element in the classroom. It's my personal approach that creates the climate. . . . As a teacher, I possess a tremendous power to make a child's life miserable or joyous. I can be a tool of torture on an instrument of inspiration.

—HAIM GINOTT

Ginott's quote helped me realize that my words and the way I said them would have more impact than anything else in creating a caring community in my classroom. So my first responsibility was to develop and practice a nurturing vocabulary. My second responsibility was to help my students understand the impact of their language and to give them opportunities each day to practice "the power of positive words." These were some of our routines:

- I stood outside the door before every class and individually welcomed each student, making sure to use his or her name and to ask a question if time permitted.
- On the first day of the school year, we had a discussion

about manners, the Golden Rule, win-win, and the power of language, and followed it up with some simple exercises.

- The students wrote a class mission statement focusing on the use of language.

- At the beginning of every class, I asked the same question: "What are we celebrating today?" The students could answer in one of four ways: share good news, talk about something or someone they were thankful for, say something positive about someone in the class, or make us laugh (as long as it was clean).

- There were signs posted all around the classroom that reminded kids about the power of their words. In addition to the "No Put-downs—Compliments Spoken Here" sign, there were others that said, "Kind words cost little, but accomplish much," "Celebrate Today!" "Celebrate Each Other!" "This Is a Caring Community," "Golden Rule Classroom," and "Win-Win Words." During the first few days of school, we discussed each one of them and how they could be implemented.

- In one section of the room was a particular set of signs. They all had one word on them, which was contained within the red circle with the slash through it. The sign in the middle said "Poison." The ones surrounding it said, "Complaining," "Moaning," "Groaning," "Whining," "Swearing," and "Gossip." I asked the kids to explain the positioning of the signs. The answer was always the same and always correct: "Doing those things is like spraying poison into the atmosphere."

- I sent at least two "Good Kid" notices home every day on students for hard work, good manners, improvement, perfect attendance, contribution to class discussion, acts of kindness, a particularly good piece of work, etc.

Please don't conclude that there was no academic learning going on in my classroom. To the contrary, I was a demanding teacher and made my students work. But I learned early in my career that they would behave better and work harder if they were in a nurturing atmosphere. My students and I created that atmosphere by consistently choosing the right words.

> *Words have the power to change a life in positive ways. They can chart a destiny. But they can also have the power to destroy a life. Be careful, and choose your words wisely. The lives of your students may very well depend on it.*
>
> —DEB BROWN

Words Can Heal in Our Schools

Words Can Heal has created a revolutionary initiative to raise awareness among the nation's youth about the power of words to hurt or to heal.

The **Words Can Heal** Character Education Program underscores the need to use language that is positive, free from name-calling, threats, taunts, slander, and teasing. The program is designed for use in schools, after-school programs, and youth organizations.

Words Can Heal trained over 100 teachers in the Los Angeles "LA's Best" program, and more than 18,000 elementary school children have received instruction in the use of positive language.

WWW.WORDSCANHEAL.ORG

No Putdowns in Our Schools

No Putdowns has been operating in our schools since 1991. Two of its primary goals are to help students increase their awareness of the power of words and to develop positive verbal skills.

Skill 5 of **No Putdowns:** "Build Up" is to teach children to replace putdowns with encouraging and supportive communication and behavior.

An independent evaluation of the **No Putdowns** program found that:

- Students acknowledged that they are more aware of their own and others' use of putdowns and the harmful impact of that behavior.
- School administrators, teachers, and students felt positive about the program and could see, hear, and feel the results.

WWW.NOPUTDOWNS.ORG

CHAPTER 13

SUPPORTIVE WORDS BOOST MORALE AND RESULTS AT WORK

In the workplace, money and fair wages are clearly important, but when it comes to long-term employee happiness and loyalty, it's truly a case of "you can't buy me love." Workers thrive, are motivated and stick around longer by recognition of a job well done—a sense that they are appreciated and included in the operation.

—BOB NELSON

"I WANT TO GIVE IT TO MY BOSS"

Several years ago I attended a weekend seminar with about fifty other people. The leader asked each of us to introduce ourselves and to say what we did for a living. He then asked each person a series of questions about his or her career. He made each person feel important by his questions, and he gave us an opportunity to learn about each other at the beginning of the day. When it came my turn, I gave my name and said that I was a teacher, an author, and a speaker. He seemed fascinated, as did many of the other people in the group, that I had written a book. He said, "I've never met an author before," while several others chimed in that they hadn't either. There seems to be some sort of mystique about authors.

The seminar leader didn't ask me any questions about my teaching or speaking, but he wanted to know everything about being an author. He asked a series of questions about writing, publishing, and the content of my first book. He then asked if I was going to write another one. I told him I'd been collecting materials for my second book for a long time and hoped to start writing it soon. He asked me what it would be about. I told him it was about the power of words, especially positive ones, and how they could bring out the best in other people.

At that point, a young woman seated near me said, "Hurry up and write it. I want to give it to my boss." This was followed by a round of laughter and a comment from another person in the seminar: "I'll take three copies. None of my bosses has a clue." More laughter, followed by several more antiboss sentiments and orders for a book that hadn't even been written yet. One of the participants said jokingly, "It sounds like all our bosses flunked the Dale Carnegie course." Then the seminar leader asked a rhetorical question: "Why do you suppose so many people in positions of leadership just don't get it?"

Actually, there *is* an answer to this question, or at least a strong theory. No matter what type of work is involved, most people start near the bottom at the beginning of their careers. In most cases, if they work hard and perform well, they get promoted. More often than not, that promotion results in managing other people. And, unfortunately, performing tasks well and leading other people can be completely different. It takes a special set of skills to bring out the best in other people, most of them having to do with effective communication, which includes choosing words wisely.

HOW MANAGERS TALK:
WHAT THE EMPLOYEES SAY

Since the topic had come up early in the day, how managers talk to their employees became the buzz. It seemed as if almost everyone in the seminar wanted to say something about how his or her boss spoke to people at work. This conversation went on during parts of the training, during breaks, at lunch, and even after the seminar ended. I heard a lot of surprising and disappointing things about the way supervisors, presidents, owners, CEOs, and other people in positions of leadership talked to their employees. (And in a recent survey, more than half of employees—fifty-five percent—said they were rarely if ever thanked for their efforts. Only thirty-five percent said they were thanked regularly.)

The people in the seminar wanted to pick my brain because they figured that if I was writing a book about how words are used, I must be the expert. But the truth was that they knew far more about words at work than I did. To begin with, I was just beginning to read and collect data about language in the workplace, and that was only a small part of the book. Second, my experiences had been limited to the academic world, and I'd received very little positive feedback from my own supervisors during my first twenty years of teaching. I had naively assumed that managers in the business world were doing a much better job in this area. But I found out differently.

Now I was intrigued and wanted to know more about how people were spoken to at work. Fortunately, I had weekly access to several people in a wide variety of jobs. My students at the University of San Francisco were in their thirties, forties, and fifties. They were in a special program designed for working adults to earn a degree in organizational behavior, which can best be described as psychology applied to the workplace. Many of them were returning to college after a number of years away, and they were hungry to learn. The goal was for them to learn to apply the theories in the textbooks to the real world of work so they could become effective managers. In the process, they had plenty to tell me about their own managers. Over the next several years, I learned that more than three-fourths of my students gave their managers poor marks for the way they talked to employees.

I taught them theory about how managers are supposed to talk to their employees, and they taught me about how most managers really *do* talk to their employees. For the next twenty years, I designed surveys, collected data, and listened to my students. The most important question in the survey—and the one the students wanted to discuss the most—was, "What are the most effective ways a manager can make employees feel valued and appreciated?" Here are their answers in order of importance to them:

What employees like to hear from their managers

1. Recognize and reward a job well done.
2. Ask for input—opinions, perspectives, suggestions.
3. Show an interest in employees—ask questions about family, activities, etc.
4. Make their expectations clear.
5. Offer to help.
6. Call employees by first name.
7. Give encouragement, express confidence.
8. Criticize gently, constructively, and privately.

My adult students also wanted to discuss the ways managers and other leaders damage morale among workers and make them feel unappreciated. Their list, again in order of importance, came out like this:

What employees *don't* like to hear from their managers

1. Gossip—unprofessional, hurts people, destroys morale
2. Ignoring employees—not talking at all to them
3. Harsh criticism, especially when done in front of peers
4. Talking down to people as if they're inferior
5. Constant complaining and focus on the negative
6. Yelling and screaming
7. Filthy and angry language
8. Threats

As these two lists of do's and don'ts began to emerge, I couldn't help but compare managers in the business world with managers in the academic world. There were no differences for the simple reason that all people, regardless of profession, have the same basic needs. They want to feel valued and appreciated, they want to be recognized for what they do well, and they want to work in an environment in which they're spoken to respectfully.

HOW EMPLOYEES TALK
ALSO AFFECTS THE WORKPLACE

My surveys were originally designed to find out everything I could about how bosses talk to workers and the effect it has on them. But research often leads to important findings beyond the initial field of inquiry, and my students reminded me that the way employees talk to and about each other is also a significant part of the work environment. Again, we came up with two lists:

*   *   *

What employees like to hear from their peers

1. Supportive, affirming language
2. A focus on what's going well
3. Clean and polite words
4. Good jokes and funny stories

What employees *don't* like to hear from their peers

1. Gossip
2. Complaining, moaning, groaning, whining
3. Angry, filthy, rude words
4. Criticism and put-downs

It doesn't take a genius to understand that what people say they like to hear and don't like to hear at work from both their managers and their peers is no different from what we all want and don't want to hear no matter where we are. What we talk about and how we talk to others, more than anything else, creates the atmosphere in which we live—at home, at school, at work, out with friends, in sports, in our places of worship. Words are powerful.

A FEW WORDS ABOUT GOSSIP

> *If we could measure the damage to corporations from gossip, it might be more than the GNP of the Third World.*
>
> —HARVEY MACKAY

There are magazines, newspapers, radio shows, websites, and television programs devoted entirely to gossip. There are people who earn huge salaries digging up dirt on other people and then spreading it around. I heard someone describe gossip recently as "our real national pastime." Gossip is, and has been for a long time, part of our culture. But that doesn't make it okay.

I knew that somewhere in this book I would need to comment on gossip but wasn't sure where to put it. I'm including it here because so many people have told me that gossip is a more serious problem at work than at any other place. It was a major issue at the school (among both students and staff members) I last taught at, it's a serious concern at work of several of my friends, and almost all of my adult students said gossip had a poisonous effect in their places of work. The Words Can Heal organization lists gossip at work as one of most serious ills in our society.

Why we gossip is not as important as acknowledging that it's a lose-lose proposition. As a Spanish proverb tells us, "Whoever gossips to you will gossip about you." It does the most damage when it comes from people in managerial positions. I was dumbfounded the first time someone told me that her boss was the biggest gossip in the company. Then I experienced it myself. One of the nine principals I taught under was the biggest gossip on a staff of more than 150. It shocked some people and hurt others. It made many feel violated, it caused friction among staff members, it ruined morale, and it drove some very good teachers out of the school. Everybody suffered because of it.

The most important question is this: Can gossip in the workplace be eliminated or significantly reduced? The answer is yes, and many companies have proved it. It's possible to create a positive workplace culture in which employees find no need to complain or gossip simply because they have better, more productive, and more enjoyable things to do. If people feel included, valued, and recognized for their work, and if they feel they're part of a team with a common goal, their energy and their conversation will reflect all these things.

There are many examples of companies, both large and small,

that have created a no-need-to-gossip environment for their employees. One is a medium-sized high-tech company right in the
middle of Santa Clara's Silicon Valley. It was founded by a friend of
mine, so during the years I was teaching organizational behavior to
adults who were working full-time, I picked his brain as often as I
could. One of the simple things he and his partners did when they
started the company was to establish a corporate culture that was
win-win in every way possible. This was communicated clearly to
the employees, and they were asked for input in helping create it.

Two employee suggestions have had a profoundly positive effect on the company ethos for many years. The first one is called
"Good News Swapping" and the other one is called "Good Gossip." Both were made at an open meeting after being asked, "What
kind of corporate culture do you want to work in?" Good News
Swapping means talking about what is going right in the company
and what is good in the lives of employees. Good Gossip means
that employees say positive things about each other whenever they
have the opportunity. At the same time, the founders created an
avenue for expressing concerns, dealing with problems as they
arose, and taking suggestions from the workers. These simple
strategies have withstood the test of time, the company is still
thriving, and the employees still call it "a great place to work."

BRINGING OUT THE BEST:
WHAT THE EXPERTS SAY

Managing other people is both an art and a science, and fortunately there's a bounty of good materials available to anyone who
wants to be an effective leader. There are books, tapes, and semi-
nars offered by many of the leading experts, such as Ken Blanchard, Stephen Covey, Spencer Johnson, Tom Peters, Warren
Bennis, Bob Nelson, the Dale Carnegie company, and several others. It's not my intention to try to add anything to their research

and findings, but it might be helpful to summarize and condense them. They're remarkably similar to what my working adult students kept telling me each year.

There are three things that successful managers consistently do that have a positive effect on both worker morale and production:

1. They let employees know they're valued

Too often employees have the feeling that they're out of the loop and that the boss doesn't even know their names. There are a number of simple ways good managers address this problem. One of them was suggested many years ago by Tom Peters and Robert Waterman in *In Search of Excellence: Lessons from America's Best-Run Companies*. They called it "management by walking around," and it proved to be as powerful as it was simple. After reading the book, many leaders in the business world made it a point to get out of their offices more often, learn names, talk to employees, ask questions, get input, and let workers know they're valued. Since the most basic need we all have, whether at work or not, is to feel as if we matter, this little bit of human contact, if done regularly, went a long way toward improving morale and production.

2. They recognize and praise employees

Too many managers make the same mistake parents and teachers make: They catch people doing something wrong far more than catching them doing something right. Whichever behavior gets recognized the most will be repeated the most often. More than sixty years ago, Dale Carnegie advised us to, "Give the other person a good reputation to live up to." Catch employees doing something well, and then watch them do it again.

Stuart Levine and Michael Crom, then the two highest executives in Dale Carnegie & Associates, Inc., summarized the power of positive recognition at work in, *The Leader in You:*

> *All people, from the president of the most successful cor-*
> *poration to the clerk at the supermarket bottle return,*
> *want to be told they're doing a first-rate job, that they're*
> *smart, they're capable, and their efforts are recognized. A*
> *little bit of recognition—a dash of encouragement at just*
> *the right moment—is often all it takes to transform a*
> *good employee into a great one.*

Surveys consistently indicate that most employees, regardless of their position or line of work, place recognition of a job well done as one of their highest needs. Bob Nelson, who's written books on the subject of rewarding employees and trains managers worldwide, lists positive recognition as the number one motivator at work. He describes it this way: "full appreciation for work well done, expressed directly by managers personally or publicly." He suggests that "Every leader needs to make it a daily habit to acknowledge everyone who is doing a great job."

3. They help employees grow

Good managers are good teachers and coaches. When they do need to correct someone, they do it privately, gently, and constructively. Rather than focus on what's being done wrong, they help employees discover ways to improve their performance while expressing confidence in them. It's helpful when managers share some of the hard-earned lessons they learned from their own mistakes while moving up in the company. The best managers are there with supportive and encouraging words even in the most trying of times.

> *The process of criticism should begin with praise and*
> *honest appreciation.*
>
> —DALE CARNEGIE

The WHALE DONE! Response

Praise people immediately.

Be specific about what they
did right or almost right.

Share your positive feelings
about what they did.

Encourage them to keep up
the good work.

FROM *WHALE DONE!*
BY KEN BLANCHARD, THAD LACINAK,
CHUCK TOMPKINS, AND JIM BALLARD

CHAPTER 14

ENCOURAGING WORDS
ENHANCE PERFORMANCE
AND FUN IN SPORTS

ARE YOU A GOOD SPORT?

Cheer good plays made by either team.
Don't talk trash or goad opponents.
Don't yell at teammates for making a mistake.
Congratulate your opponents and teammates.
Have fun!

—MICKEY RATHBUN

SPORTS AND SPORTSTALK

While sports are important in many countries, nowhere are they more prominent than in the United States. Our culture consists primarily of family, politics, economics, entertainment, faith, and sports. Which one occupies most people's time and conversation? A significant number would say it's sports. Not only are there three or four sports going on all the time, there are newspapers, magazines, and radio and TV shows entirely devoted to them. We can watch sports twenty-four hours a day, and some men can't talk enough about them. One national TV sports show advertises itself this way: "Hey! Four idiots sittin' around talkin' about sports. What could be better than that?"

While there's a lot of sports viewing and a lot of talk *about* sports, there's also a lot of talk *within* sports. That's what this chapter is about. This talk within sports comes primarily from parents, coaches, and the athletes themselves. And they can be just as powerful—for good or for bad—as words spoken anywhere else. My comments here have to do with all levels of sports: youth, school, college, professional, and adult recreational sports.

PARENTS' WORDS IN YOUTH SPORTS

At one point during a soccer game, the coach called one of his seven-year-old players aside and asked, "Do you remember how we talked about good sportsmanship?" The little boy answered, "Yes." "So," the coach continued, "I'm sure you know that when a foul is called, you shouldn't argue, curse, yell at the referee, or call him a peckerhead." The little boy nodded. The coach added, "And when I take you out of the game so another player can get a chance to play, it's not good sportsmanship to call your coach a 'dumb-ass,' is it?" Again, the little boy nodded. "Good," said the coach. "Now go over there and explain all of this to your mother."

No, soccer moms don't usually say things like this, but the story does make a point: The language of parents plays a bigger role in youth sports than most of them realize. We read every year about some of the most bizarre examples of parent behavior: loud swearing, threatening (and even injuring) a coach or umpire, verbally abusing opponents and their own kids, etc. Fortunately, these are not indicative of most parents with kids in youth sports. But this type of behavior has been a problem for a long time. Only in the last few years has it been addressed in a proactive and effective manner.

Sports psychologists have played a big part in reducing the amount of verbal abuse in youth sports. In recent years there have been a number of valuable studies done, and the findings have been published in magazines and on the Internet. Many organizations have incorporated these findings into their philosophy, mission, and goals. For instance, many of the Little League and youth soccer leagues now require all parents, coaches, and players to sign an agreement regarding positive behavior and language before the start of every season. The results have been phenomenal. All people need is a reminder and a commitment to be "good sports."

COACHES ARE TEACHERS

All coaches at each level of competition, whether they realize it or not, are teachers. Their primary responsibilities are to pass on their knowledge, promote skill development, and bring out the best—to get the people they lead to perform at the highest level. These are no different from the responsibilities of a first-grade teacher or a university professor. The most fundamental tool used to achieve these ends is language. The choice of words and how they're spoken are as critical to athletes as they are to students.

When sports were first developing in this country, many coaches didn't see themselves as teachers. They compared themselves more to generals leading their troops into battle. That's how the boot camp style of training, the in-your-face screaming, and the filthy language and name-calling in athletics originated. Unfortunately, there are too many coaches at all levels who still use these techniques. But the good news is that there have been tremendous strides forward in the coaching profession in recent years.

The Positive Coaching Alliance

One of the most promising developments took place at Stanford University in 1998 when the Positive Coaching Alliance was created. Aware that there were more than four million volunteer coaches working with more than forty million athletes between the ages of five and eighteen, a distinguished group of psychologists, coaches, teachers, and athletes founded the PCA to make sports a more positive experience for kids, coaches, parents, and fans.

Two of the main tenets of of the PCA mission have to do with how coaches talk to their athletes:

1. A Positive Coach understands that compliments, praise, and positive recognition fill "emotional tanks."
2. A Positive Coach . . . encourages players to make a commitment to each other, and to encourage one another on and off the field.

At the time of this writing PCA, through its training programs, had impacted more than 250,000 young athletes. Its goal was to raise that number to one million by the year 2005.

A TALE OF TWO COACHES

I was fortunate to attend the University of San Francisco on a basketball scholarship. I arrived two years after USF had won back-to-back national championships, so the school was then recognized as a basketball power. My experiences playing there were both good and bad, each determined by the type of coaching I received.

My coach for the first two years was Ross Giudice, a former great player who had been on a national championship team himself in the early 1950s. Ross was a kind, gentle, and positive person both on and off the basketball court, and his influence as both a teacher and as a coach remains with me to this day. If ever there was a coach who knew how to get the most out of his players, it was Ross. He did this by focusing on our strengths and encouraging us to give our best under all circumstances. He had a special way of letting us know that he believed in us.

At best, I was a college athlete of average abilities. I didn't have the necessary physical tools, such as quickness and jumping ability, to earn a spot in the starting lineup, but I did have some assets that could help the team. I had a great attitude, always hustled, and had a soft and accurate shooting touch. Ross reminded me often of my strengths, let me know I was a valuable member of the team, and put me into every game with words of confidence and encouragement. He helped me shake off mistakes, applauded my successes, and always had something good to say about our effort at the end of every game, whether we won or lost.

The thing that was most important to me at that time was knowing that my coach had confidence in me and appreciated my contributions to the team. Ross's affirming comments had a powerful effect on my performance both at practice and in games. I always wanted to live up to the faith he had expressed in me. Ross was a positive and encouraging coach who never swore and yelled only when he needed to get our attention. When I coached basketball in high school several years later, I used Ross as my role model. My coaching strategies weren't as good as his, but my players were always treated with respect and appreciation.

My last two years of college basketball were the opposite of my first two. Ross left coaching to go into business full-time, and the university hired his replacement shortly afer the season ended. The new coach came onto campus, held a press conference, and said wonderful things about the university, the basketball program, the players, and the previous coaches. Then he made a point of talking to all the returning players, both as a group and individually. He told me he had heard great things about me, knew that I would continue to contribute to the team, and looked forward to having a good coach-athlete relationship with me. That was the last positive thing I ever heard come out of his mouth.

When the season started the following year, we immediately learned that things were going to be different. Our new coach's primary means of communicating with his players were screaming, swearing, negativity, harsh criticism, name-calling, biting sarcasm, threats, and humiliating players in front of their teammates. He didn't talk like this to all the members of the team. A few of the stars escaped his wrath, so he took out his frustrations on the rest of us. And some of us were more favored targets than others. If he detected a little sensitivity in any of his players, he would go in for the kill.

He once sent me into a game with these words of encouragement: "Now don't f——up!" I went into the game, caught a pass, stepped on the out-of-bounds line, and was immediately replaced by one of the starters. I might have set an NCAA record: quickest in/out ever—less than two seconds. And what did I hear when I came back to the bench? At the top of his lungs, and while spitting, he screamed, "I told you not to f——up!"

A few weeks later we were playing a home game, and a player on the other team put an excellent move on me, went around me, and scored an easy basket. The timing was about as bad as it could have been. It occurred just before the end of the first half. The coach began his halftime talk with these unforgettable words in front of all my teammates: "Urban, you can't play defense worth sour owl sh——!" I'm unfamiliar with that substance, but I was pretty sure he meant that my defense stunk.

Another time he got me after the game was over, again in front of my teammates. Even though I was an excellent free throw shooter with a high percentage, I missed an important one near the end of the game, which we lost. As any athlete would, I felt terrible. It would have been nice to receive a comforting word from my coach at about that time. But in the locker room right after the final buzzer, he said to me, "All I wanted from you was one f—ing free throw. You can't even give me that? You're pathetic." There were countless more of these kinds of incidents involving both me and other players, many worse than the ones I've described here.

Two coaches, two different styles of communicating with his players. Which one brought out the best in his players? Which one set the better example? Which one was the better teacher? Which one left us with good memories? Which one was a good role model?

EVEN THE PROS NEED A LITTLE ENCOURAGEMENT

Does an NBA all-star who is young, handsome, rich, and famous need to be told by his coach that he's playing well? Apparently, the answer is yes. In 1999, Chuck Daly was considered one of the best coaches in the NBA, and Penny Hardaway, one of Daly's players on the Orlando Magic, was one of the stars of the league. Hardaway hit a mild slump in his shooting and the team lost three in a row. Daly said little to him, so Hardaway concluded that the coach had lost confidence in him. In an interview with *The New York Times,* Hardaway said he had probably jumped to the wrong conclusion from the coach's silence. "I know we make all this money and everything, and you wouldn't think some of us need reinforcement. But you want to hear from your coach that you're doing well, even at this level."

Daly, known as a players' coach, solved the problem by having a private, heart-to-heart talk with Hardaway. He reminded him that he was a great player, told him to have fun, and invited him to come and talk to him any time he wanted. Hardaway broke out of his slump and the Magic went on a winning streak. Hardaway said later, "I'm not saying that was the main reason we haven't lost since, but it definitely helped. He let me know how important I was to this team."

A few years before that, Tim Wallach, then the third baseman for the Los Angeles Dodgers, was ready to hang it up. Once a great hitter, his average had been below .230 for two seasons in a row. But Reggie Smith, a first-year batting coach on the team, wouldn't let Wallach quit. He encouraged him and told him that he could get his "stroke" back with a little extra work. So during the off-season, Smith worked with Wallach three times a week. This is the way Wallach described those sessions: "Reggie was positive from day one. Regardless if I felt I was having a bad day and was struggling, he'd find something good about what happened. You just don't see that often. People tend to work off the negatives, but Reggie wouldn't do that, and he wouldn't let me do it either."

Wallach finished the year with twenty-three home runs and a .280 batting average. He gave all the credit to Reggie Smith's coaching and encouraging words. Tim Wallach in the Major Leagues, and Penny Hardaway in the NBA—both needed the same thing every Little Leaguer, high school athlete, and college athlete needs: recognition, praise, and encouragement from the coach.

A TALE OF TWO TEAMMATES

Almost as important as the words of a coach are the words of a teammate. At any level of competition, athletes need someone on their team to "pick them up" when they're down, to encourage them during tense moments, and to congratulate them for making a good play. Athletes thrive on this kind of positive feedback.

I'll use two examples from adult recreational sports, but the points that are made here could apply to athletes of all ages and all ability levels. These two happen to come from what is known as Senior Softball. Please don't conclude that these are wobbly old men who can barely walk. These are highly skilled and dedicated athletes past the age of fifty who compete for a world championship in their sport just as their counterparts do in tennis, golf, track, soccer, and other sports.

My friend Ray lives on the East Coast and plays Senior Softball at the same level I do in California. One of our goals is someday to play against each other in a world championship tournament. We keep up with each other's team's wins and losses, and because we're men, we compete with each other for the highest batting average. When we were playing in the fifty to fifty-five age division a few years ago, we swapped stories about teammates who had a powerful impact on our respective teams. Unfortunately, Ray had a teammate who used his mouth to destroy a team. I was the lucky one. I had a teammate who made me and several of my teammates better and made playing on the team a lot more fun.

"Mr. Big"

Ray had started out on a team that wasn't very good, but within a few years it had vastly improved by picking up better players. In the third year, it landed one of the superstars in his area, and the team figured it had a real shot at qualifying for the world championships. This great new teammate was an outstanding hitter and outfielder, and his play significantly improved the team's win-loss record. But within a month things began to deteriorate. The new player, whom Ray referred to as "Mr. Big," had little respect for his teammates, their abilities, or their feelings. When they made an error in the field or made an out in a crucial situation, he was always in their faces to remind them that they had screwed up. When *he* made a mistake or struck out, no one said anything.

Mr. Big also frequently criticized the manager's decisions, yelled at umpires, and complained about some of the rules and many of the fields. In short, he was a downer. His constant negative comments took the fun out of playing for several of his teammates, and three of them quit the team. He told the manager, loudly enough for others to hear, "We need to get rid of a few more guys if we're going to be any good next year." At the end of the season, Ray and three other guys also left the team. Ray told me, "The guy was like a cancer on the team. He ruined it. We play to have fun, but couldn't have any with him around."

Freddie

At the same time, I was on a team that had also been improving, and we picked up three new players. All were good athletes and very nice guys. One of them, Freddie Santos, was the greatest teammate I've ever had in any sport, and that covers a period of more than fifty years. What made Freddie so special? It was what he said to his teammates and how he said it. Besides being a great athlete, he was Mr. Positive, the Energizer Bunny, and the Encourager all rolled into one.

When we were in the field, Freddie was always talking, always hustling, always keeping us on our toes. When we were at bat, he was always expressing his confidence in us and shouting encouragement. If someone made an error that cost a run, he was there to say something like, "Shake it off; we'll get it back." Freddie's positive energy and positive words had a profound effect on our team. I can't remember going to bat a single time without Freddie telling me that he just knew I was going to get a big hit. I joked to our manager that having Freddie around had added at least fifty points to my batting average. When I checked my stats at the end of the year, I found out that my average had in fact gone up fifty-four points over the previous year. Do I really think Freddie's words had something to do with this? Absolutely! Every athlete, at least once in his or her career, should be so lucky as to have a teammate like Freddie. And every athlete should try to *be* a teammate like Freddie.

WORDS IN WOMEN'S SPORTS

The number of girls and women participating in youth, school, college, professional, and adult recreational sports is now more than one hundred times what it was only thirty years ago. In addition, there are more co-ed sports than ever before, especially at the recreation level, in tennis, softball, soccer, basketball, volleyball, water polo, running, and others. Is the language used by both athletes and coaches in women's and co-ed sports any different from that used in sports that are exclusively male? Yes. Do male athletes and coaches have anything to learn about the importance of words in sports from females in athletics? Yes.

I realize that there are some macho jocks and coaches who will scoff at this, but the truth is that the words heard among women athletes and coaches are cleaner, less critical, and more encouraging. It doesn't mean women are less competitive, and it doesn't mean that a female coach or athlete won't yell or get angry on occasion. What it does mean is that women are more likely to use language in sports that creates a supportive atmosphere. They tend to choose their words more carefully.

I have a friend who has extensive coaching experience with both boys and girls at the high school level. He said the girls made him a better coach for both. Initially concerned about not wanting to hurt the girls' feelings, he learned to use more constructive language and to say it in a gentler tone. He then discovered that the same technique made him more effective with the boys. He also found that girls, in general, were better teammates. They were less likely to criticize another player and more likely to give encouragement and to acknowledge outstanding plays. He felt that the atmosphere and the chemistry on his boys' teams improved significantly when he taught them the importance of a teammate's words.

The college coaches I spoke to had come to essentially the same conclusions. They said women athletes are less critical and demanding of each other and more encouraging than their male counterparts. Male coaches and players are more likely to get on each other verbally in the heat of battle, then leave it behind when the game is over. Most female athletes don't do this because of the emphasis they place on the social dynamic of team sports. They want to be close to their teammates, so they're less likely to say something that might be offensive. The male coach of a nationally ranked women's volleyball team said this is one of the most enjoyable aspects of his job. The positive words of his women athletes have also taught him to be a better coach. Together, he and his athletes create an atmosphere that is conducive to teaching, learning, competing, and being part of a team.

These same principles apply to co-ed sports, especially at the adult level. My wife is what some might call a "tennis nut." Cathy loves the sport and plays whenever she has the chance, both with women and in mixed (co-ed) doubles. I asked her if the men and women talk differently when they're competing together. I wasn't surprised at the answer. In general, the men are more likely to correct a partner after a mistake. She said, "When I make a mistake, I know what I did wrong, so I don't need a partner pointing it out to me. What I *do* need to hear at that time is a little encouragement. That's what good teammates do." In any sport, at any age level, regardless of gender, that *is* what good teammates do. They encourage each other, just as my friend Freddie did on the softball field.

Words of Wisdom from a Legendary Coach

Who's the most respected person in the history of all sports in the United States? If this question was asked in a national survey among knowledgeable people, I'm confident that John Wooden, the former great basketball coach at UCLA, would be named most frequently. Not because he's in the Hall of Fame as both a player and as a coach, and not because he won ten national championships, but because of what he brought to the entire world of sports—wisdom, principles, and character.

I think his book *Wooden: A Lifetime of Observations and Reflections On and Off the Court,* written with Steve Jamison, should be required reading for all athletes, coaches, and parents involved in sports. In fact, I would also highly recommend it to anyone *not* involved in sports. Bill Walton, one of Wooden's greatest players, said his coach taught him a lot more than basketball: "The skills he taught us on the court—teamwork, personal excellence, discipline, dedication, focus, organization, and leadership—are the same tools that you need in the real world. He wasn't teaching us about basketball, he was teaching us about life. John Wooden taught us how to focus on one primary objective: Be the best you can be in *whatever* endeavor you undertake."

Here are some of Coach Wooden's thoughts about the importance of words in sports:

- Control your temper and don't use profanity.

- Leadership is the ability to get individuals to work together for the common good and the best possible results while at the same time letting them know they did it themselves.

- I feel that hard public criticism embarrasses people, antagonizes them, and may discourage them from being receptive to your message. It is counterproductive, whether it's on a basketball court or in a business establishment.

- Today's showboating runs contrary to what the spirit of the game is all about. . . . Trash talking, pointing at other players, and taunting them, all belittle your opponent and show a lack of respect.

- The individuals who aren't playing much have a very important role in the development of those who are going to play more. They are needed, and you must let them know it. . . . I tried to let them know they were important, that they were valued.

- Seek individual opportunities to offer a genuine compliment.

- Your reaction to victory or defeat is an important part of how you play the game. I wanted my players to display style and class in either situation—to lose with grace, to win with humility.

A good coach will make his players see what they can become rather than what they are.

—ARA PARSEGHIAN

Research has shown that positive coaching can increase an athlete's self-esteem and self-confidence, which results in more enjoyment from participating, which causes a child to be more likely to continue playing.

. . . Providing a positive and favorable playing environment should be the goal of every youth sports organization leader, coach, and parent.

—POSITIVE COACHING ALLIANCE

WWW.POSITIVECOACH.ORG

Good coaching may be defined as the development of character, personality, and habits of players, plus the teaching of fundamentals and team play.

—CLAIRE BEE

PART FOUR

TWO FINAL THOUGHTS ON THE POWER OF POSITIVE WORDS

We can make it a point to express ourselves in a harmonious, cheerful, tactful, and caring manner.

—SIR JOHN TEMPLETON

CHAPTER 15

KIND WORDS
IN WRITING BECOME
LASTING TREASURES

It only takes about three minutes to write a note, fold it, stick it in an envelope and mail it, but the power of it is awesome.

—WANDA LOSKOT

WHEN WORDS ARE BETTER IN WRITING

Most of this book is about what we say to each other during the course of everyday conversation. But we also write words, and while it's slower than talking, what we say on paper can have a powerful and lasting impact. Notice that I said *on paper*. While e-mail is a valuable tool for certain types of communication, I'm referring here to the old-fashioned, personal handwritten note or letter.

A number of experts in the fields of business, communication, etiquette, and human relations have been enthusiastically promoting the use of the handwritten notes for many years. Many of them point out that these kinds of notes have a greater impact now than they ever did. We've become accustomed to hearing from others instantaneously via phone, fax, or e-mail, so the handwritten note stands out. It says someone took the time, the thought, and the effort to add a personal touch.

Here's what five authorities have to say about the power of words in writing:

Norman Vincent Peale, author of *The Power of Positive Thinking* and several other books: "The purpose of writing inspirational notes is simply to build others up because there are too many people in the demolition business."

Tom Peters, management guru and author of several books on excellence in business: "We wildly underestimate the power of the tiniest personal touch. And of all personal touches, I find the short, handwritten 'nice job' note to have the highest impact."

Mary-Ellen Drummond, president of Polished Presentations International: "Personally expressing your gratitude and acknowledging the good in someone through a handwritten note can strengthen, repair, or build relationships far faster than the speed of an e-mail message. Don't misunderstand me. I love e-mail, but when I want to reach out in a significant way, it's best to do it in a personal note or even a postcard. It shows you personally took the time to think about the other person."

Al Franken, humorist and best-selling author: "Ask yourself this: doesn't it seem more sincere and extraordinary that someone would take the time to send you a personal handwritten note?"

Margaret Shepherd, author of *The Art of the Handwritten Note:* "A good handwritten note on the right occasion is a work of art. It says to the reader, 'You matter to me, I thought of you, I took trouble on your behalf, here's who I am, I've been thinking of you.'"

WORDS IN WRITING CAN CHANGE LIVES, EVEN START CAREERS

Scott Adams, the creator of *Dilbert,* one of the most successful comic strips of all time, says that two personal letters launched his career and dramatically changed his life. Being a professional cartoonist had been a dream of his for quite some time, but he had no idea about how to get started. Then one night he watched a PBS-TV program about cartooning, and he got some ideas. He wrote to the host of the show, Jack Cassady, and asked for his advice. Much to his surprise, he heard back from Cassady within a few weeks in the form of a handwritten letter. In it, Cassady provided answers to all of Adams's questions.

Cassady encouraged Adams to give it a go and advised him to not be discouraged if he received early rejections. Adams got inspired and submitted cartoons to two national magazines. He was quickly rejected by both with form letters. Not following Cassady's advice, he got discouraged, put his materials away, and decided to forget cartooning as a career. About fifteen months later, he was surprised to receive yet another letter from Cassady, especially since he hadn't thanked him for his original advice.

In this second letter, Cassady wrote: "I'm dropping you this note to again encourage you to submit your ideas to various publications. I hope you have already done so and are making a few bucks and having some fun, too. Sometimes encouragement in the funny business of graphic humor is hard to come by. That's why I am encouraging you to hang in there and keep drawing." Adams says he was "profoundly touched" by this gesture, especially since Cassady had nothing to gain by writing either letter. He acted again on Cassady's encouragement, but this time he stuck with it and obviously hit it big. Adams says, "I wouldn't have tried cartooning again if Jack hadn't sent the second letter."

As *Dilbert* grew, Adams came to appreciate the enormity of Cassady's two simple acts of kindness put into writing. He did thank Cassady this time but felt he had been "given a gift that defied reciprocation." Adams added, "Over time, I have come to understand that some gifts are meant to be passed on, not repaid. All of us know somebody who would benefit from a kind word. I'm encouraging you to act on it. For the biggest impact, do it in writing. And do it for somebody who knows you have nothing to gain."

The Top Ten Occasions for Handwritten Notes

Although there's no limit to the number of reasons for writing a personal note or letter, below are some of the occasions on which people most appreciate receiving them. Keep in mind that I'm suggesting a personal, handwritten note in each case, not a store-bought card with someone else's words.

1. **Thank-you notes.** There never was, and never will be, a substitute for the old-fashioned, handwritten thank-you note. Nothing expresses your appreciation more than a personal note that comes from the heart.

2. **Expressions of sympathy.** When someone else suffers a loss, receiving a personal note is one of the gestures that offer the most comfort. These are the hardest to write, but sincerity will always come through and be appreciated.

3. **"Thinking of you" messages.** Receiving these are among the great joys of life. They come out of the blue and remind us that we have good friends who literally do think about us even when there's not frequent contact.

4. **Congratulations.** We all like to be acknowledged for our achievements, no matter what they are. Whether it's graduating, getting a job or a promotion, having a baby, buying a house, or reaching some other milestone in life, it always feels better when someone congratulates us in writing.

5. **Letter of apology.** We've all been hurt or wronged by another person, and we've all caused some hurt in others. A good starting place for the healing process is a heartfelt letter of apology. It usually leads to a cure.

6. **Notes in the workplace.** Former Ford Motor Company chairman Donald Peterson was well-known for his practice of giving positive, handwritten notes to associates almost every day. Peterson said, "The most important ten minutes of your day are those you spend doing something to boost the people who work for you."

7. **Wishing someone well.** We all have changes in our lives that often become significant turning points. Whether we're moving, changing jobs, or going on a trip, the encouraging and kind written words of a friend always enhance the experience.

8. **Resolving conflicts.** A lot of personal conflicts never get resolved because neither person wants to make the first step, or doesn't know how. An excellent way of doing this is to write a short and simple note inviting the other person to join you in the search for a solution.

9. **Empathy for hard times.** In addition to losing loved ones, we suffer a lot of other hardships in life. It's very comforting to get a note from someone who's been

through something similar and takes the time to write words of support.

10. **Reminders of love and friendship.** It's always nice to receive a card or note on special occasions such as birthdays, holidays, etc. But it's even better to receive one when there's no obligation or "reason." These kinds of notes that simply say, "I value our friendship" or "I love you," are almost as much fun to write as they are to receive.

THE FOUR S'S OF EFFECTIVE PERSONAL NOTES

Fred Bauer, an author who had Norman Vincent Peale for his boss and mentor for many years, wrote a compelling piece in *Reader's Digest* a few years ago called "The Power of a Note." Peale and many other well-known people had made personal note writing part of their daily routine, and they had enriched the lives of thousands through them. Bauer says that effective notes have these four things in common:

1. **Sincere:** No one wants their sails filled with smoke.
2. **Short:** If you can't speak your piece in three sentences,

   you're probably straining.
3. **Specific:** Complimenting a business colleague by telling him "good speech" is one thing; "great story about Warren Buffet's investment strategy" is another.
4. **Spontaneous:** This gives them the freshness and enthusiasm that will linger in the reader's mind long afterward.

WHEN PERSONAL NOTES BECOME TREASURES

The main reason so many people keep photographs is that they want to preserve memories of special times and special people. The same is true of personal, handwritten notes. Many of them touch us so deeply they're never forgotten. They're also usually saved. When they're read a year or several years later, they continue to lift our spirits and evoke wonderful memories. Notes from children and grandchildren are among the most treasured, but there's a wide variety of other personal notes that also earn special places in our hearts.

As a high school teacher for many years, I was amazed at how much teenagers and their parents treasured short written notes for being acknowledged in a positive way. Our school district printed thousands of "warning notices" every year for teachers to send home when a student had bad attendance, bad grades, a bad attitude, or bad behavior. Is it any wonder that the students called them "bad kid notices"? They also claimed that the only time the school sent something home was to tell the parents that they had a "bad kid."

I learned early in my career that the school district had a "bad kid notice" but it didn't have a "good kid notice." That problem was easily solved. I asked a friend on the staff who was far more skillful with a computer than I was to make up a "good kid notice" in our school colors. Twenty minutes later I had hundreds of them. Since I usually had about 170 students, and most of them did something good every day, I figured I would need a lot of them. They were fun to fill out and mail because I knew they would be win-win-win: the student, the parents, and the teacher. But I greatly underestimated the impact these little notices would have.

A couple of days after sending out the first few notices, I received a phone call from the mother of one of my senior boys.

She was literally sobbing, and her words are etched indelibly in my mind: "Oh, Mr. Urban, you have no idea how happy this makes us. Curtis has been at that school for four years and has received many warning notices, but this is the first time we've ever heard anything good about him. We will treasure this notice because someone finally found something good in our son." I didn't think I had done anything heroic, but this mother and her son thought I had. Curtis thanked me personally the next day in school and got all choked up in the process. Their responses gave me a preview of what was to come. Although not everyone responded, a high percentage of them called me and wrote to me with a similar message, and almost all the kids personally thanked me. Virtually all of these simple notices were saved, some even framed.

Among my own treasure chest of personal notes are ones from my three sons, my mom, my wife, colleagues (especially when I retired from teaching), students, their parents, and people who have written to me about my first book. One of my all-time favorites came from Crystal, a senior in my psychology class in the late 1990s. Crystal was a teacher's dream: polite, conscientious, curious, insightful, hardworking, and kind. I was shocked when I learned that she was living in a group home because neither her mother nor father, who were divorced, wanted her. How could anyone, especially her parents, not love this kid? She was a special student who also became a dear friend, and she joined our family for Thanksgiving dinner the year she was in my class. She was truly a blessing in my life.

On the last day of the semester, Crystal wrote something to me that went straight to the heart and has remained there ever since. She was the last one in the class to turn in her final exam and even continued to work on it after the bell had rung for lunch. She finally turned it in, gave me a hug, and told me she'd come by to see me often the following semester even though she wouldn't be in my class. That comment alone made me feel wonderful. A few hours later, when I got to her final exam, I realized that she needed extra time because she had written a letter to me and attached it at the end. The entire letter was beautiful, but it was the last two sentences that penetrated more than I thought words on a piece of paper could. She wrote, "We don't get to pick our parents when we come into the world. But if we did, I would pick you as my father." As you might imagine, it brings tears to my eyes just to write about it. Mark Twain said he could live for two months on one good compliment. This one will last a lifetime.

I share this not to make myself look like a hero but to give you a real-life story about how powerful the right words in writing can be. We all have the power to be a Crystal in someone's life if we just take the time to write a note expressing our love or appreciation.

> *In a world too often cold and unresponsive, spirit-lifting notes are springs of warmth and reassurance. We all need a boost from time to time, and a few lines of praise have been known to turn around a day, even a life.*
> —FRED BAUER

A handwritten note is like dining by candlelight instead of flicking on the lights, like making a gift instead of ordering a product, like taking a walk instead of driving. Handwritten notes will add a lot to your life. You can still use the telephone or the web for the daily chores of staying in touch, but for the words that matter, it's courteous, classy, caring, and civilized to pick up a pen.

—MARGARET SHEPHERD

CHAPTER 16

POSITIVE WORDS
ADD JOY TO LIFE . . .
BUT ONLY IN THE LIVING

Do not save your loving speeches
for your friends till they are dead;
Do not write them on their tombstones;
speak them rather now instead.
—ANNA CUMMINS

DON'T WAIT UNTIL THEY'RE GONE
TO EXPRESS YOUR FEELINGS

One of the greatest regrets of my life has to do with something I *didn't* say but should have. The person I should have said it to was Dr. David Kirk, one of my English professors at the University of San Francisco. What I should have told him was that he was a fabulous teacher and a wonderful person, and that what he taught me about writing and about teaching had a profound and lasting effect on me. They say a great teacher's influence lasts forever. Dr. Kirk was proof.

I think about him every time I sit down to write. I also put into practice the simple yet powerful techniques he taught me. I feel his influence not only when I write a book but also when I write an article, a letter, or an e-mail message. I also felt his influence throughout my teaching career. He had a passion for his profession, was a great storyteller, and when he needed to criticize, he always did it gently and constructively. He was a great role model for an aspiring teacher and writer.

During my undergraduate years, and since then, I've praised Dr. Kirk literally hundreds of times. But there's one problem—the praise never went directly to him. It was *about* him but was communicated to other people. This is a common mistake most of us frequently make. We like, admire, or appreciate someone, but we tell a third party instead of the person who's getting praised. Why do we do this? Because it's safer. Most of us haven't been taught how to tell people how much we appreciate them. So we tell someone else instead.

When I heard that Dr. Kirk had died, I was hit by a double dose of sadness. First, because of his passing. Second, because I never told him how much he had contributed to my life. While this is something that I'll always regret, I did learn from my sin of omission. I vowed then that if someone came into my life and made a positive contribution, he or she would hear about it—not from someone else but from me.

I share this story because I know countless other people have done the same thing I did and what I *didn't* do. I encourage you to look around. You'll find a lot of people who enhance the quality of your life. Tell them. Most of them need to hear it once in a while. You'll make two people feel really good: the other person and yourself. And the more you do it, the easier it will become to do again. It's truly a win-win proposition.

The greatest weakness of most humans is their hesitancy to tell others how much they love them while they're still alive.

—O. A. BATTISTA

THE MEMORIAL SERVICE LESSON

For many years I was a classroom teacher who tried to connect the real world to my academic subjects. Therefore, I was always on the lookout for life lessons that could be brought into my teaching. The best one of my career occurred more than thirty years ago when I was trying to teach high school seniors to use more life-affirming language, to build each other up instead of putting each other down. This was always a challenge but well worth the effort.

In the spring of 1972, I had a wonderful group of kids in my afternoon psychology class. They were polite, energetic, motivated, and fun to teach. There was only one thing that bothered me about them. They, like many teenagers, seemed to have some inherent need to put each other down. They often did it in a joking manner, but the person on the receiving end didn't really think it was all that funny. The put-downs weren't malicious; they were just insensitive and often hurtful.

My psychology class was an elective, so the kids were in the course by choice. I called it the "psychology of personal growth and development" and always promoted the course as one in mental health. My mission was to help these students tap in to their potential for rich and rewarding lives. I wanted to bring out the best in them. The put-downs were inconsistent with both my goals and the type of atmosphere I was trying to create, so I needed to address the issue.

We started class every day in the same manner. I would ask, "What are we celebrating today?" They could share good news or share something or someone they were thankful for. It took only a few minutes, but it was powerful and always helped us get off to a positive start. I asked the kids, knowing what the answer was, if they liked the way we began class. They all agreed that it was a good way to begin and that they actually looked forward to it. I shared with them my concern about how the put-downs were inconsistent with what our goals were.

Their responses didn't surprise me. They said things like, "Oh, we're just kidding," "That's just what teenagers do," and "We don't mean anything by it." I asked, "Do you like being on the receiving end of a put-down, even if the person is 'kidding'?" A few said it didn't bother them, but most agreed that it could be hurtful and/or embarrassing at times. I asked them if they realized that putting each other down was the exact opposite of what we could be doing. I suggested that in addition to sharing good news and things and people we're thankful for, we could also say something complimentary and affirming about someone in the class.

You should have heard their reaction to this idea. "No way!" was the first thing I heard. In a polite way, they went on to tell me the following things about my suggestion: "Kids don't really say things like that," "That would be really embarrassing," "It would be so awkward."

I realized they were correct. Kids *didn't* say those kinds of things, and because they weren't used to doing it, it would, indeed, be embarrassing and awkward. I wanted to come up with an analogy, something they learned to do comfortably after working their way through the awkward and embarrassing stage. I thought of learning to ride a bike, since they had all gone through that. I asked if they all remembered their earliest experiences with a two-wheeler. They did. I asked if they had gone through an awkward and embarrassing stage with the bike before they became comfortable and confident with it. They had.

I said, "Because no one's ever taught you how to give compliments or affirm one another, and because you've never really done it, I can understand how it would be uncomfortable at first." I asked them if they felt good when someone recognized them in a positive way. Naturally, the answer was yes. I asked if affirming other people would be a good social skill to have if it could be done comfortably. Again, the answer was yes. Then came the more challenging question: "Would it be worth working through

the awkward and embarrassing stage to get to a comfort zone in
affirming others?" There was some hesitation on this question,
but most agreed that it was worth a try. Since I had never done
this with kids before, I wasn't sure what to expect, but I did know
that it wouldn't be easy and it wouldn't happen quickly. I was
committed, no matter how long it took. I said, "Okay, we'll start
tomorrow."

The following day I was at school but realized that I wouldn't
be in my afternoon psychology class because I was leaving early to
attend a memorial service. I asked another teacher to cover my
class and to tell my students that we would pick up with the
affirming words challenge on the following day. The memorial
service was at a large church in a nearby community. It held about
twelve hundred people, and there were at least eight hundred
attending the service. My wife and I had never been in this
church before, so we were on unfamiliar ground. We took a seat
near the front where we saw some friends.

The service had a surprising start. The pastor came out from a
side door, picked up a cordless microphone, and walked right
down the center aisle to the front row. He looked happy at a time
that seemed to call for sorrow. Then he boomed out with a big
smile on his face, "Today is a celebration of life!" And he meant it.
He went on to explain *why* it was a celebration. Bob, the
deceased, had lived a full life, had been a great family man, was
generous, had started a successful business and treated his
employees well, had many friends, etc. The pastor went on to say
that Bob was also a believer and that he was now in a better place
than all of us were. He convinced me and many others that we
were there, indeed, to celebrate Bob's life. The remainder of the
service was also upbeat, focusing on some positive Scripture readings. It was also very short, which surprised me. These kinds of
services usually lasted about an hour, and this one was about half
of that.

Then the pastor surprised us again by grabbing his cordless

mike and coming back to the front row. He said he had kept the service short because he wanted Bob's friends to help in the celebration. He asked if anyone would like to share a memory about Bob. At about this time, the body posture of most of those eight hundred people became very rigid. Speaking in front of large audiences is still the number one fear among Americans. But the man sitting next to me didn't have that fear, and he immediately raised his hand. The pastor was there within seconds and handed him the mike. He paid a beautiful tribute to Bob. He also relaxed many of the other people, and now hands were going up all over the church, and the pastor was literally running from person to person so he could give them the mike. This went on for about twenty minutes, and it truly was a celebration of life.

While the tributes to Bob were going on, I couldn't help thinking about the conversation with my students the day before about how hard it was to say nice things about people. Here was a large group of adults doing it and not having a single problem. But then it dawned on me why. It was safe to say all these nice things about Bob because he wasn't there. I wondered how many of these people told Bob these things while he was still alive. I answered my own question: probably none.

I've told this story many times all over the country. A few years ago a teacher in the Tulsa area asked me afterward if she could share an anonymous quote that seemed to fit in with my story. Always delighted to pick up new materials, I assured her that she could. What she shared with me is classic:

> *A single rose*
> *is of greater value to the living*
> *than an entire wreath is to the dead.*

Think about that for a minute. Which would you rather do, give a friend who's still alive a single rose or take a wreath of them to his or her memorial service? Which one would bring greater joy to the receiver? Which one would bring greater joy to the giver? How about if we changed the quote a little?

> *A single kind word*
> *is of greater value to the living*
> *than a whole bunch of kind words*
> *at a memorial service.*

On my way home from the service that afternoon, I was already figuring out how I could turn this experience into a life lesson to share with my students who were so fearful of saying something nice to another person. I couldn't wait to get back into that psychology class and share the story with them. When the time came, I asked them if anyone remembered what we had been talking about two days before. They all did, and one of them crystalized their feelings when she said, "We were talking about how hard it is to say nice things to people." I said, "I have a story for you."

I proceeded to tell them about the memorial service in great detail. When I was done, I asked them a simple question: "How many of those people who said nice things about Bob at his service had told him the same thing when he was still alive?" No one answered verbally. They just shook their heads. They had come to the same conclusion I had.

At about this time, Nancy, sitting in the last row in the middle of the classroom, got an idea. She started waving her hand like a third grader does when she wants to be called on. High school seniors are usually too cool to do this, but Nancy was fired up. I said, "Nancy, you have an idea?" She said, "Oh, Mr. Urban, I know how you can get us to say nice things about each other, and it won't even be uncomfortable." I said, "Great! Let's hear your plan."

Nancy says, "Bring a casket into the classroom. Put it up in the front and open the top half. We'll take turns sliding into it." She then demonstrated how she would lie on her back with her eyes closed and her hands folded on her stomach. Nancy had quite an imagination. She then held up her yellow highlighter and said, "You could be the pastor, Mr. Urban, and this could be your mike. You just ask if anyone has something they want to say about me, and then you pass it around as they raise their hands. The neat thing is that I'll get to hear it all. I'll be in there listening and totally digging everything they say."

Nancy's flash of brilliance conjures up several pictures, all of them very funny. Try to imagine this going on in a public high school classroom. The kids were laughing and so was I, but her suggestion created a problem. I wasn't sure if she was kidding, being serious, or a little bit of both. If she *was* serious, I didn't want to discount her idea. But I also didn't want a casket in my classroom.

I stumbled over this dilemma for a few seconds and then said what was probably the dumbest thing that ever came out of my mouth in thirty-five years of teaching. I said, "That's a great idea, Nancy, but I don't know where we'd get a casket." Teachers laugh uproariously when I tell this because they know that saying that to a bunch of teenagers is like issuing them a challenge. I was lucky I didn't have six caskets waiting outside my door the next morning. But what I said was even dumber than I had originally thought. As soon as it came out of my mouth, I looked down at Walt, who was sitting right in front of me. Take one guess at what Walt's dad did for a living. That's right. He was the local mortician. Walt was a real laid-back kid and pondered the situation for a minute, then raised his hand slowly. He said, "That won't be a problem, Mr. Urban. Which model do you want?"

We got a little off track at that point because the kids wanted to know about all the models, including the one Walt called the "Mercedes" of the line. And of course, they were astonished at the prices. But we eventually got back on track, and I asked them the following questions:

- Does the memorial service story make a point?
- Do we have to wait until someone dies to say something nice?
- Can we do it without a casket or other props?
- Are you willing to take some steps outside your comfort zones?
- Is there someone in this class who deserves an affirming word?

They got the point. And we added affirmations to our good news and thankfulness for the rest of the school year. Was it awkward and embarrassing as they had predicted? You bet it was. But they worked their way through it just as they had when they learned to ride a bike, and they became very good at building each other up instead of tearing each other down. I continued to teach kids about the power of words and how to affirm for the next thirty years. And I always introduced it with the memorial service story. The moral of that story is obvious: Don't wait until they're gone to express your feelings.

THE LAST TIME

Many years ago I attended a lecture at a local college about communication skills. I don't remember the name of the speaker, but I do remember vividly one thing he said. It fits perfectly with the memorial service story and is great advice for all of us.

Talk to your friends and family members as if it's the last time you ever will.

If you were going to die soon and had only
one phone call you could make, who
would you call and what would you say?
And why are you waiting?

—STEPHEN LEVINE

PART FIVE

SUMMARY
AND
CONCLUSION

We cannot afford to underestimate the importance and power of our words.

—JEFF OLSON

Never lose a chance of saying a kind word.

—WILLIAM MAKEPEACE THACKERAY

Summary

Kind words have the power to

Cheer us up when the world is getting us down

Honor us for our achievements

Cause us to giggle and laugh

Restore our faith in the goodness of humanity

Bolster our self-image

Inspire us to give our best

Let us know someone cares

Lift our spirits

Warm our hearts

Improve our moods

Heal our wounds

Acknowledge our hard work

Bring out the best in us

Boost our confidence

Support us in tough times

Celebrate our triumphs

Comfort us in time of sorrow

Make us feel like we count

Help us to believe in ourselves

Encourage us when we need an extra little push

Remind us about what's right and good in the world

Supply us with a burst of energy

Tell us we're appreciated

Surprise us with joy in unexpected times

Teach us valuable lessons

Uphold us during our darkest hours

Give us the recognition we deserve

Point out the reasons for being thankful

Show that others have faith in us

Brighten our days

Enrich our lives

CONCLUSION:
ALWAYS HAVE SOMETHING GOOD TO SAY

A few years ago I received one of those special letters that always touch a teacher's heart. It was from Bill, a former student who was about to graduate from college. He wrote to tell me that I had taught him something of great value, something that had stayed with him throughout college and would remain with him for the rest of his life.

It's always nice to receive positive feedback, but this was especially touching because Bill had been one of the greatest students I ever had the privilege of teaching. He reminded me that in his first few days as a student in my class he thought "that affirming language stuff was kind of corny." But he gave it a try and soon became a convert. He said the lessons on language helped him in four ways: First, he became aware of the awesome power our words can have, so he developed the habit of choosing them more carefully. Second, he learned to look for the good, especially in other people, and he found opportunities everywhere to comment on it. He said, "Now I always have something good to say." Third, he found out that once he got started, it became natural and easy to use life-affirming language. Fourth, every time he made someone else feel good, he couldn't help feeling better and happier himself.

My hope and my prayer is that reading this book will do the same for you.

Set a guard over my mouth, O Lord;
Keep watch over the door of my lips.

—PSALM 141:3

Let no one come to you without leaving happier and better.

—MOTHER TERESA

Do not let any unwholesome talk come out of your mouths, but only what is helpful for building others up according to their needs, that it may benefit those who listen.

—EPHESIANS 4:29

ACKNOWLEDGMENTS

There are times when the words "thank you" seem hopelessly inadequate, simply because they can't express the depth of gratitude one feels. This is one of those times. There are no words that can fully convey the heartfelt appreciation I have for the three individuals and the two teams of people who've made the writing and publication of this book possible. But I need to try.

Tim Hansel—As stated in the text, Tim planted the seeds of this book more than thirty years ago when we were teachers on the same faculty. I had never met anyone who so consistently looked for the good, found it, and celebrated it. He was especially skillful at finding the good in other people and letting them know about it. Thank you, Tim, for enhancing my life and for teaching me the life-affirming power of positive words.

Caroline Sutton—Little did I know when I sold my first book to Simon & Schuster that I was about to form a friendship that would immeasurably enrich my life both professionally and personally. Professionally, Caroline's insight, superb language skills, and creative suggestions enhance the clarity of my writing. Personally, her sense of humor and her joy of living enhance the quality of my life. Thank you, Caroline, for being the best editor/friend an author could ever have.

Joe Durepos—For many years I said that I would never sign with a literary agent. That changed when I met Joe. His integrity, work ethic, accessibility, and vast experience in the book industry have proved invaluable. His sense of humor and kind heart make him the complete package. In addition, he does what I don't want to do—he handles all the business negotiations required to publish a book, and he does it with the touch of a master. Thank you, Joe, for being a great agent and a treasured friend.

The Simon & Schuster team—I had several concerns when I sold my first book to this large and well-established New York publishing house. Could the people who work in such a high-powered place be enjoyable and personable? Would I still have a say in matters related to the book now that it belonged to a major company? Would phone calls and e-mails be returned? I'm happy to say that the answer to all of these questions was a resounding yes! It's been one of the best and most personally rewarding professional experiences I've ever had. No author could be happier with his publisher. Thanks to the following people who've made this special relationship possible: **Marcella Berger, Marcia Burch, Laurie Cotumaccio, Shelly Davis, Christina Duffy, Chris Lloreda, Debbie Model, Trish Todd,** and **Jeff Wilson.**

The Character Education team—Some of the finest people I've ever known have become friends and colleagues in just the past ten years. Each of them is a leader in the Character Education movement and has made a significant contribution to the lives of teachers, parents, and kids throughout the country. Each is also a consistent user of positive words and has made a significant contribution to the contents of this book. Thank you **Charlie Abourjile, Marvin Berkowitz, David Brooks, Deb Brown, Jerry Corley, Matt Davidson, Anne Dotson, Tom Lickona, Helen LeGette, Sandy McDonnell, Linda McKay, Robert Rabon, Nancy Reed, Kevin Ryan, Eric Schaps,** and **Phil Vincent.**

ABOUT THE AUTHOR

HAL URBAN holds a bachelor's and a master's degree in history, and a doctorate in education and psychology from the University of San Francisco. He has also done postdoctoral work at Stanford University in the psychology of peak performance.

For thirty-five years he was an award-winning teacher at both the high school and university levels. His first book, *Life's Greatest Lessons,* was selected as "Inspirational Book of the Year" by *Writer's Digest.*

Since 1992, Dr. Urban has been speaking nationally and internationally on positive character traits and their relationship to the quality of life. He gives keynote addresses at national conferences, conducts workshops with educators, and talks to students of all ages. He also speaks to parents, church groups, service organizations, and people in business.

Information about his lectures and workshops can be obtained at his website: **www.halurban.com**

He can be reached by mail at:
    P.O. Box 5407
    Redwood City, CA 94063
and by telephone at: 650-366-0882